SALMON FLYFISHING

SALMON FLYFISHING

The Dynamics Approach

FRANCIS T. GRANT

SWAN·HILL
PRESS

DEDICATION
To Gylla Lawrence

Copyright © 1993 by Francis T. Grant

First published in the UK in 1993
by Swan Hill Press an imprint of Airlife Publishing Ltd

British Library Cataloguing in Publication Data
A catalogue record for this book is available from the British Library

ISBN 1 85310 394 2

Printed by Livesey Ltd, Shrewsbury, England

Swan Hill Press
An imprint of Airlife Publishing Ltd
101 Longden Road, Shrewsbury SY3 9EB

Contents

Acknowledgements

I would like to thank all who helped in creating this book. I am grateful to those who read, and made comments (however improper!) at various stages, to those whose enthusiasm provided moral support, or who gave practical assistance by, for example, taking photographs, and to any whose names have been taken in vain. My special thanks to Pam Woodward who deciphered my scribblings to produce the typescript.

As for those who encouraged me to write it in the first place, they have only themselves to blame!

Introduction

Even at the age of three I was fascinated by salmon. I remember being taken to lunch at Abersnithack, which was a lodge rented by some of my father's fishing tenants. They had caught a couple of grilse that morning, and these were lying on a large plate in the hall. I was entranced by these beautiful silver fish, and kept running out of the dining room to stroke them. This was an obvious source of irritation to the grown-ups, who insisted on washing my hands every time I did it. Clearly, from their point of view, an energetic three-year-old with hands covered in fish slime was not a particularly attractive prospect.

Within a year or two, I had progressed to catching trout in the burn, using a handline bought from the village shop, and a fly begged from my father, or worms extracted from under rocks and logs. I also became adept at catching trout in a landing net, when they foolishly sought shelter in the nooks and crannies under the waterfalls. At that age, I was not allowed on the river bank unaccompanied, and adults generally had better things to do than to waste time taking small boys fishing. In those days, children were to be seen and not heard.

However, I had an idyllic early childhood, dabbling in burns and ditches, in an Aberdeenshire uncorrupted by motor cars and television. But it was not till the age of eight that I caught my first trout of over a pound in the River Don, and my first salmon followed a year later. By the time summer holidays from prep school had arrived that year (1965), I had learned to swim the required 50 yards, and I was now allowed on the river bank by myself.

In the late 1960s and early 1970s the lower reaches of the Don were grossly polluted by all manner of sewage and effluent from paper mills and bacon factories. As a result, salmon runs were small compared with those enjoyed by leading rivers at the time. However, there were enough for me to catch a few every year during the school holidays. I was also fortunate to be sometimes invited for a day's fishing on the Dee. At that time, this held huge stocks of salmon, and I often saw more fish in a few minutes then, than I now see in a day, or even a week.

It was not till after I left school and went to university in 1973 (to study Marine Biology), that I began to get more regular access to the Dee. This was through the kindness of Gylla Lawrence, who at the time was a great friend of my aunt, Elspeth Waddington, who had been the wife of another famous salmon fisher, Richard Waddington. Gylla very kindly invited me, first of all to share a rod for a day or two, and then later to fish for a week, and then a fortnight at Ballogie each year.

Regular access to a good beat on the Dee provided both the opportunity, and the spur, to improve my approach to salmon flyfishing. Initial success was probably due to no more than persistence, and the ability to cast an extra yard or two. Soon I began to think more about what I was doing, and why. I also started to experiment occasionally with what are usually regarded as less conventional techniques, initially with nymph style fishing, and latterly with the dragged surface fly in the early 1980s. By then, my catches at Ballogie were sometimes reaching slightly embarrassing levels, and explanations began to be sought. My replies of preparation, presentation and persistence were considered to be not quite as informative as my inquisitors would have liked! I had also decided to try to broaden my experience of fishing under different conditions, by taking the occasional week elsewhere. In the middle 1980s, I was usually managing to obtain about four weeks of serious, or semi serious-salmon fishing each season.

Trying to explain my approach was difficult, for it was not easy for me to find the words that would make clear how I controlled the speed of my fly, what influenced my choice of method, and why I felt that the need for this control over the fly was so important. By about 1987 I had begun to rationalise my description of what, for me, was an instinctive process of judgement, into the beginnings of a more coherent argument. I called it the dynamics of salmon fly presentation. The argument suggests that at any given water temperature, there is a wide range of salmon fly sizes that may be successful, and that the success of any particular size will depend on its being moved at the appropriate speeds relative to the water and to the fish.

I chose the word 'dynamics' to describe the factors that influenced the way that I presented the fly, because of vague memories of schoolboy physics. Dynamics, I recalled, was a branch of mechanics that dealt with motion and the relative movements of objects under the influence of forces. It seemed appropriate, for the motion of the fly was affected by the current, and how I manipulated rod and line. The salmon, too, would expect different sizes of prey organism to behave differently at varying water speeds and temperatures. It also emphasized the need for positive action by the angler.

During some of my long summer holidays as a student, I worked as a hotel gillie. This provided me with a number of opportunities. By watching while others fished, I learned techniques and skills that have proved very useful over the years. Perhaps more importantly, I also learned how not to do some things, and of the need for a stealthy approach, especially on smaller rivers. Sitting on the bank, overlooking the river for long periods, as the gillie must, I saw many fascinating examples of how salmon and trout behave. Donning a wet suit, to cut branches and young trees growing out from the bank in deep water, enabled me to see at first hand the astonishing speed and agility of the salmon, and to realise just how clumsy and slow are our own movements in the same element.

After graduating in 1977, I worked as a fish farmer until early 1979, when I came to the conclusion that there had to be easier methods of earning a living, although I had added considerably to my knowledge of fish behaviour. I wanted regular holidays, and some evenings and weekends to myself. I also thought that it might be nice to be warm and dry, rather than cold and wet. So I decided that I would probably have to have an office job, and out of the only ones I could think of, stockbroking sounded more fun than banks or insurance. Chameleon-like, I changed my skin into a pinstripe suit, and turned into a stockbroker.

I survived for eleven and a half years pretending to be a stockbroker, but in November 1990, redundancy caught up with me, as with so many others in the city.

Almost unanimously, my fishing friends greeted the announcement with joy. 'Oh good, you can get on with the book now', they said. Previously, I had always managed to counter their suggestions that I write a book, by saying I was too busy. 'If you don't write it now, you may never have such a good opportunity again. You have got to let other people know how you do it', they persisted, clearly unsympathetic to the plight of the unemployed.

'But you all get driving lessons from me', I replied, referring to my detailed instructions on tactics for various pools at different times.

'That's not the same at all', they said. 'How will anyone else know? What will we do if anything happens to you, like you get squashed under a bus or something?'

'Probably break out the champagne, I expect', I replied sourly. I had run out of excuses, and they knew it.

Having yielded to the pressure of their superior judgement, I have tried to explain in writing what I meant by preparation, presentation and persistence, including the ideas that underlie my dynamics approach. I hope my thoughts will interest the dedicated salmon fisher who is prepared to make the necessary mental and physical effort to achieve success. I would also like to encourage those with less experience to broaden their understanding of the fish and the sport, so that they can enjoy using a more imaginative range of techniques, thus increasing both their competence, and the pleasure they obtain.

Part 1 — The Fish

The salmon's activity, or metabolic rate, is directly controlled by its body temperature, which is approximately that of its surrounding environment, water. The lower the water temperature, the more sluggish it is, and the higher the temperature, the more active it becomes. In understanding the behaviour of salmon, the linkage between water temperature and the fish's behaviour is very important. Just like people, salmon are all different individuals, and their behaviour will show a range of different responses to any one set of conditions. So, even in the coldest water, for example, some salmon will be more active than others, and therefore more likely to respond to, say, a faster-moving lure, or one that is higher in the water, or smaller in size than the usual presentation.

As the water temperature rises, it has another effect that many anglers forget. The amount of oxygen that can be dissolved in the water becomes progressively smaller as the temperature increases. This means that just when the fish needs most oxygen to support its high metabolic rate, there is less available to it in the water. This is what creates the upper limit of water temperature above which the salmon cannot survive, because it will not be able to extract sufficient oxygen to meet its metabolic demand. In Britain, this upper limit is usually a few degrees over 70°F, although in rivers with appreciable quantities of suspended, or dissolved organic matter (creating its own biochemical oxygen demand) the limit may be lowered. It has also been suggested that salmon in some rivers are more tolerant of high temperatures than in others. Whatever its absolute level, the fisherman will find that salmon become increasingly reluctant to take a fly at temperatures approaching 70°F. If, however, the water temperature suddenly falls to the mid 50sF, having been stuck in the middle to upper 60sF for a while, this can produce a brief period of hectic sport. For a day or so, the increase in available oxygen, without any change in water level, seems to make every fish in the river wake up, even those that have been lying dormant for weeks in the pools. Some of my largest catches have occurred in these conditions.

As far as the angler is concerned, the other important factor in the fish's behaviour is the degree of appetite suppression. As the salmon moves from salt to fresh water on entering the river, it has to change the way it regulates the composition of its body fluids. In the sea, the salmon has to try to conserve the fresh water in its body, while excreting the salt. When it enters the river, the process has to be reversed, and it must conserve the salt in its body while eliminating the fresh water. This changeover, possibly in association with the onset of sexual maturation, seems to trigger a process of appetite suppression.

There is a biological need for appetite suppression in the returning salmon. If they fed as voraciously in the river as they did in the sea, every small fish in the river, including all the salmon parr, would soon be consumed, and the salmon as a species would disappear.

The appetite suppression is not total, nor is every salmon affected to the same degree. In some the appetite is very little suppressed, and these fish are promptly caught (or hooked and lost, or pricked a few times!) by anglers soon after they have entered the river, which is one reason why fresh fish are reckoned to be such good takers. The fish that are left tend to be the ones that show the strongest suppression of appetite, and these become the so-called residents, resting in the pools, becoming gradually staler by the day.

Anyone who can recall the high days of early spring fishing in the 1960s will realise that the degree of appetite suppression does not always increase with the length of time a fish is in fresh water. Opening day on the Dee (1 February) frequently saw bonanza catches, with individual rods taking dozens of fish. These salmon had not appeared in the beat overnight, or even in the previous few days. In many cases, they had been in the river for a couple of months, perhaps entering fresh water in early December. Yet a proportion of them were ready takers, showing that despite their length of stay in the river their appetites had not been totally suppressed.

Another factor that may influence the suppression of appetite is the degree of acidity of the water. Many people have commented that acid, peaty water in a river that is usually clear will tend to put the fish off the take. However, salmon in rivers that are normally acid and peat-stained even at low water do not appear to be so affected, which might suggest that there is some variation in tolerance of acid water conditions between the populations of different rivers. Sea water is slightly alkali (pH around 8.2), while most rivers are slightly acid with a pH of less than 7, and occasionally as low as 5. (A pH of 4.5 or lower may be lethal to adult salmon with increased fry mortality occurring below pH5). It is therefore possible that the appetite suppression mechanism may also be affected by the change in pH as the fish moves from salt to fresh water, and by changes in the degree of acidity in the river itself.

Some older anglers believe that nowadays salmon are not such ready takers as they were prior to the mid 1960s. If this is so, it might be linked with the growing problem of the acidification of Britain's rivers and lakes due to acid rain. This has been correlated with the rapid increase in upland afforestation since the war, but real public concern did not become apparent till the beginning of the 1980s. It is probably not coincidental that this was about 5 years after the Government abolished the subsidy on the spreading of lime on agricultural land. Since most of this lime was spread on upland pastures, it effectively buffered some of the very acid rainfall on the higher ground until the scheme was stopped. If a similar scheme could be reintroduced, perhaps under the politically more acceptable tag of an environmental support payment, it would be interesting to see not just the resulting improvements in fish numbers and water quality, but also whether anglers reported a return to more freely taking salmon. This would support the idea of some link between the acidity of the water, with its related increase in dissolved aluminium, and the suppression of appetite in the returning salmon.

I know that many authorities have said that salmon never eat in fresh water. Any angler who has caught a salmon on a worm, and found that it had swallowed the hook down into its stomach, will disagree. It would be better to say that the majority of salmon seldom eat in fresh water.

If salmon never ate in fresh water, they would never be caught by anglers, and it would be a complete waste of time to fish for them. (I know there are some disappointed men who maintain that salmon fishing is a waste of time anyway!) However, I cannot imagine that anglers' lures are the only things to be attacked by salmon in fresh water, and that other creatures must also be likely to suffer from their attention occasionally. This is born out by frequent observations of salmon rising to take flies on the surface of the water, not just in rivers but in still waters as well.

Not only are different fish affected by the suppression of their appetites to varying degrees, but the individual may be more affected at some times than at others. This is perhaps why one is more likely to catch a previously identified 'resident' at dusk (or dawn), after it has refused every offer throughout the day. It is only at dusk, when most predators' instincts (including the salmon's) are at their keenest, that its appetite suppression could be overridden by the stimulus of the angler's fly. The suppression will also be reduced by other factors. If the fish leaves, or is going to leave a long favoured lie, for any reason, this can prompt a resumption of taking behaviour.

Some salmon leave their lies at dusk, and appear to go for a cruise around the pool; "stretching their legs", as a friend of mine so aptly describes it. They sometimes venture into quite thin water at the throat, or tail, of the pool, and are then often vulnerable to the well presented fly. If even the staunchest of residents is pushed out of his lie by heavy water in a spate, he can often be caught with ease. When I fished at Ballogie in the middle to late 1970s, the pools often held large numbers of resident salmon, which became well known to us, watching their regular jumping, day after day, in the same place. If one was caught, it was easily identified.

I like to think of the salmon's occasional taking response while its appetite is supposed to be suppressed, to be similar to that of a person lying in bed, feeling vaguely unwell, and definitely off his food. If offered a plate of mince and potatoes, he will refuse. However, if someone walks into the room, says "Here, catch!" and lobs a grape at him, his hand will go up automatically and catch the grape without a thought. It is exactly the same with the salmon. The right kind of stimulus will trigger the fish's predatory behaviour into overriding its lack of desire to eat.

Other factors that can overcome appetite suppression include aggression and playfulness. As the season progresses, the sexually maturing salmon feels the nearness of the spawning season, and particularly among male fish, which will have to fight for access to the females on the redds, increasingly aggressive behaviour will lead to them taking a snap at any strange object intruding into the territory of their lie. At times, late in the season, this can make them so ridiculously easy to catch that they are not a fair test of the angler's skill.

Salmon certainly show a high degree of playfulness at times. I have seen them roll quite deliberately on top of a fly, or hit it with the underside of their chins, in what looked like an attempt to drown it. In such cases they usually come up with their mouths closed, and quite obviously make no attempt to engulf the lure. On other occasions I have seen them suck the fly in, and blow it out again, without ever closing their mouths, sometimes repeating this action several times. I can recall one or two resident fish repeating this behaviour day after day (in the same lie), as the weeks of the season progressed. When I was a gillie, I usually had a 'pet' fish that did this somewhere on the beat, most seasons.

I have also seen salmon come up and quite deliberately give the lure a thump with their tails. I remember watching from the bridge at Aboyne while a man was spinning in the pool below. He was using a yellow belly minnow which was clearly visible at all times. There was a group of about thirty or forty salmon, restlessly circling in the pool, and which all obviously intended to be on their way upstream again very soon. They all ignored the minnow as it passed overhead, until one of them suddenly moved rapidly up towards it from about three or four yards downstream. However, instead of taking the lure as I expected, it turned just short, and then swam parallel with, and about a foot away from the minnow for a short distance, perhaps a couple of yards, across the pool. The fish then gave the minnow a sudden hard blow with its tail and headed away downstream, where I lost sight of it. The impact was sufficient to knock the minnow two or three feet to one side in the water. I made my way down from the bridge and chatted to the angler about what I had seen. He had felt nothing, apart from a slight knock, as if the minnow had bounced over a rock. I often wonder how many other such incidents pass unnoticed by anglers blissfully unaware that a salmon has 'visited' their lure.

Fish that are running fast can often be the worst offenders when it comes to this playful behaviour with the angler's lure. Frequently they do no more than take a quick snap at the fly before immediately spitting it out again, as they continue their rapid progress upstream without a pause. When fishing with the floating line, all too often the fish, having risen, do not turn down again with the fly in their mouths. This usually leads to an infuriating sequence of plucks, pulls, lightly hooked and lost fish, which can sometimes severely damage the unfortunate angler's confidence. I prefer fish that are moving upstream more slowly, and pausing regularly as they travel. They seem to take the fly much more positively, and consequently tend to be far better hooked.

One other possible, and here I heavily stress the possible, mechanism that might overcome the suppression of appetite in red fish, is hunger. It is no more than an idea, but one that I think is worth considering. Why should a ripe, and very black, hen fish ever take a fly? After all hen fish do not need to display the same aggression on the redds as the cock fish. Some early run spring fish may spend nine months in the river before spawning. During all this time they have been converting muscle and fat reserves into energy and roe or milt. In this process they may lose a quarter of their body weight before they spawn. It is just possible that they may start to feel hungry again towards the end of their fast, for they have a considerable need to restore some of this lost energy. After spawning, the appetite suppression mechanism is 'switched off', for everyone knows of the voracious hunger of the kelt. (It is probably no coincidence that salmon parr seem to go into hiding at low water temperatures, otherwise large numbers might be consumed by kelts in the early part of the year). It might just be possible that the mechanism may start to be 'switched off' a little prematurely in some fish, before they have spawned. I know that I am not wholly convinced by the argument that the black hen fish, which takes my $1/2$" Hairy Mary tube on a floating line in late October, is merely preparing to defend a redd, that she has not yet made, against potential predators. Whatever the reason, I wish she would leave my fly alone, because I do not want to catch her. I worry too much about inflicting injuries that might prevent her spawning.

The angler should also be aware of the conditions in which salmon like to run, for he will wish to have a steady stream of new arrivals appearing in his beat. In early spring, salmon prefer the waters of the river that they are about to enter not to be too much colder than the sea. In a long cold winter, when the river may be frozen for extended periods, the fish may be reluctant to enter further than the estuary, and many will not even want to come that far, preferring to wait offshore, where they are less vulnerable to seals. However, within a few days of a thaw setting in, these fish waiting offshore may suddenly appear with a rush. Conversely, very high river temperatures may also act as a barrier to prevent fish entering in summer from the cooler waters of the sea.

In some rivers, fairly high water may be needed to encourage the fish to come in, and these are usually where the estuary is very shallow, or where the river mouth has obstructions, such as sand bars. However, once in the river salmon are not likely to need so much water to move up. Granted certain individual obstacles such as waterfalls, or weirs, may need a particular minimum flow before they can be ascended in safety, but in general, salmon will run fastest upstream in a low to medium water height, especially when the water temperature is above the low

40sF. Under these conditions, salmon can travel very fast indeed, and pass right up through the lower and middle stretches of the river without stopping, especially if there is a lack of high quality holding water. This can be infuriating for those paying high rents to fish these beats, knowing that hundreds and sometimes thousands of fish have passed through each day, while they have been lucky to catch a single fish, if anything. Worse still, they will be aware of reports telling of large bags from the upper beats. If the salmon cover 50 or 60 miles in a few days, which is often the case when sea liced fish are caught in the upper reaches, they obviously have not spent much time resting in the pools on their way up.

High water is a different matter. It undoubtedly stimulates the fish to run, but they do not travel so fast. The reason for this is fairly straightforward. When a river is chugging along bank high, its average water speed may be two or three times what it was at a lowish level. At best, the fish is therefore likely to cover only half or a third of the distance with the same effort. So it moves upstream more slowly, pausing frequently to rest on the way, providing much better chances for anglers.

However, a very big flood, of the kind that will drown surrounding fields under several feet of water, can wash large numbers of fish downstream. These fish sometimes appear to be reluctant to resume their upstream journey for a while after the flood. For example, there was just such a torrential flood on the Dee in February 1990, and it wrought havoc in many of the best pools, either by ripping away yards of bank, or by depositing thousands of tons of shingle. I arrived a couple of weeks after it to fish at Birse, and found a disappointing lack of salmon. Many fish that had been evident in the beat before the flood had dropped downstream to the lower reaches of the river. There they remained, semi-dormant in the pools, till the water really warmed up at around the end of April. They then departed at speed for the upper reaches. This resulted in very disappointing catches for many beats that year, especially for those that are often reckoned to be among the best of the middle sections of the river.

I have often seen it claimed that salmon somehow know when a drought is coming, and will run up to the headwaters of the river unusually fast, and unusually early, when this is so. Alas, this romantic notion of the salmon's forecasting abilities is pure conjecture, and unsupported by fact, other than the most randomly inconsistent coincidence. Take 1985 as an example. I had two sessions on the Dee, one at Birse in March, and one at Ballogie at the end of April/beginning of May. On both occasions, I had to struggle to pick up the odd fish, despite the visible evidence of large numbers travelling rapidly up through the beats. It was particularly irritating while I was at Ballogie, because there were consistent reports of big catches, and the pools being 'full of fish', on all the beats upstream of Aboyne, only a few miles above us; while from Aboyne downstream the reports all told of very few fish being caught, and larger numbers being lost. There had not been much snow that winter, and the river was usually at a lowish level. The 'experts' said that this movement of the salmon was a sure sign of coming drought, and a lack of water in the summer. The summer of 1985 turned out to be one of the wettest I have ever experienced, with consistently high water levels from June till October. So much for the experts' predictions! The fish were running fast early on because they had the right conditions of water height and temperature, and for no other reason.

Very cold water will obviously tend to slow the fish down because it reduces their metabolic rate. Similarly, if there is a rise in water temperature, it can induce the fish to run. If large numbers of fish have been lying quietly in the pools of the lower reaches of the river since early spring, when the water warms in late April or early May, they will begin to make their way upstream once more, without needing any change in the level of the river to encourage them. It is purely the influence of the warmer water.

In February or March, when water temperatures are in the mid 30sF, the fish do not usually run more than a few miles in a day. Very often they will not start to move till after the fractional warming of the water around 11 or 12 a.m.

Low water temperatures can prevent salmon from ascending certain obstacles such as weirs, falls or heavy rapids. These obstructions can only be passed once the water temperature has risen to a level at which the fish's metabolism can work sufficiently fast to produce enough energy in a short period to enable the fish to get up. Different barriers may have different temperatures at which they become passable. A moderate fall may be climbed at a temperature of 42°F, whereas a steeper one might not be passable till it has warmed to 52°F. Thus the arrival of salmon in the upper beats can often be controlled by water temperatures.

As they travel upriver, salmon will pause in different places for varying lengths of time, from a few seconds to several months. Depth of water and speed of flow can be important factors influencing the duration of a fish's stay in any one place. Brief pauses will often be made in water that is shallower or faster than that preferred for long stays.

Good holding water, where the fish will often remain for weeks, is usually fairly deep, normally at least six or eight feet even at low summer levels, when the flow may be reduced to a trickle. However, fish may rest for a day or two in water that is only three or four feet deep, before moving on, but such lies tend to be rapidly forsaken if the level of the river starts to drop. Sometimes fish will tend to pause briefly, perhaps for a few minutes only, or half an hour, in water less than a couple of feet deep. This seems to happen most often when the water is warm (over 60°F) and the fish are running very fast.

It should be remembered that the salmon is a shoal fish, and the presence of residents in a pool will encourage others to pause there, temporarily, as they make their way up river. If there are no residents present in a pool, running fish may well swim straight up through it without stopping, which will tend to depress catches. This means that one should beware of wading too deep in times of low water, and thereby walking the fish off their lies and so sending them up out of the pool and probably the beat as well.

Many commentators have remarked on the importance of the air being warmer than the water. This is only because it usually means that the water temperature is rising, with a consequent increase in the metabolic activity of the fish, and hence the chance of a positive response to the angler's fly. The reverse is true when the air is colder than the water, which often produces a fall in water temperature and fish activity. I do not think the fish are too concerned about the air temperature, only with changes in water temperature.

Whatever the reason, I do not like large daily fluctuations in water temperature, whether up or down. On the Dee, in times of low water with an overnight frost followed by daytime temperatures into the 70sF, I have known water temperatures to vary by as much as 8–9°F in a single day. This always seems to unsettle the fish, and they seldom take well. They can be very stiff to move in the morning after the sharp overnight drop in temperature, before running rapidly up through the beat without stopping in the afternoon. I prefer the water temperature not to move by more than 3 or 4° during the day.

Other weather conditions do not appear to have a very consistent effect on the salmon. Despite many years of watching the barograph at Monymusk, I still have not formed an opinion about the way that changes in atmospheric pressure affect the fish. I have made good catches at all points of the cycle between the most persistent high pressure anticyclone, and the trough of the deepest depression. I have also had blank days at all points of the cycle as well. I suspect that the rainfall and consequent increase in river levels have a much greater impact than the rising barometer after a depression has passed.

Aside from its rather depressing effect on morale, fishing in pouring rain can sometimes be quite productive. The impact of the raindrops helps conceal the angler, the movement of his rod, and the splash of his line landing on the water, which it also helps to oxygenate. I also suspect that really heavy rain might provide a different taste to the water, which may help to stimulate the fish long before any rise in water level becomes detectable.

The wind usually has more effect on the angler than it does on the salmon, unless one is fishing in a loch, in which case it may be of major importance in determining where the fish are to be found. Under normal conditions on a river, the best wind is conspicuous by its absence. However, when fishing a small fly on a floating line in fast water, where precise control is needed, I like an offshore and upstream breeze. A downstream, offshore wind enables one to cast vast distances, but can make it nearly impossible to control the fly properly, and one often has to accept that it will fish faster than desired, and to adapt by using a slightly larger fly. From the angler's point of view, a strong wind blowing slightly upstream, and almost directly onshore, is probably the worst. If the angler is wading down the edge of a deep, wide, slow-moving dub, and trying to cast a full sinking line and heavy brass tube as far across it as he can, and this wind is accompanied by frequent showers of sleet and snow, it can be a miserably frustrating experience. However, a strong wind can be very useful at times of low water, and a good chop on the surface can be as beneficial as a rise of several inches in water levels. It conceals the angler, who will probably be fishing the pool by backing up, and will provide that essential 'life' to small flies fished near the surface.

I do not think that salmon like bright, squally weather. For the fish, this produces a rapid succession of sudden changes from light to shade, and back again, as a series of clouds are blown rapidly across the sun, or dark catspaws of wind scurry over the surface. Sudden shadows disturb the fish, for their instinctive response is to fear the approach of a predator, and to sink immobile to the bed of the river until the nature of the danger, if any, becomes apparent. Of course, more gradual changes from light to shadow are not a problem, and are often beneficial, but bright blustery weather seldom provides good taking conditions in my experience.

The effect of sunlight is more difficult to quantify. Some of my biggest catches have occurred on days of unrelenting glare, with a bright sun, and not a cloud in the sky. Of course, I have also used just those conditions as an excuse for not catching anything! I do not like the sun shining down the pool, either directly or slanted from either bank, if I am fishing with the floating line The fish is facing upstream, and as it moves forward and rises in the water to take the fly, it will be travelling straight into the dazzling glare. Also, the shadow of the leader will fall towards the fish when the sun is behind it, shining down the pool. When it is shining up the pool, it will make the shadow of the leader fall away from the fish. In very bright conditions, I have frequently seen salmon rise up through the water to take a fly, and then turn away at the last second. I am sure that they were disturbed by seeing the leader, or its shadow. So if there are not too many rocks or other obstacles, it is probably wise to use a slightly finer leader in bright sunlight. However, the presence of the sun, and its angle on the water, matters far less when using the sunk fly. Indeed even half an hour's bright sunlight in the early part of the season can be a positive bonus, for it may provide just that fractional warming of the water, which might be needed to stir a fish into action.

Bright sunlight has less effect in high water than it does in low water. High water usually means a faster current, and a more turbulent surface, which will reduce the amount of sunlight penetrating the water. The fish may also be lying deeper, and the heavier stream might mean that they have less time to make up their minds as to whether to attack the fly or not. This contrasts with the often slower, shallower, and calm surface conditions of low water, which can provide the fish with the opportunity to make a more leisurely approach to the fly.

While I do not think that salmon have such acute vision in the dark as brown trout or sea trout, they can certainly see well enough to make their way up river, and to take a fly, especially when the water is warmer than the mid 40sF. On even the darkest night, with an overcast sky and no moon, you may have a very good chance if you are fishing the vee at the tail of the pool at the same time as a group of fish arrives. Other good places after dark are up at the throat of the pool, or where the flow is concentrated around a shoulder of rock or other obstruction.

At night, I prefer to use quite a large fly on a floating line, as I think the fish see it better against the surface, than they do a deeply sunk fly. I have even caught them when there has been such a thick mist coming off the water, that I could not see the surface, scarcely a yard away from my peering eyes. If you are at the bottom of a steep bank, where you cannot beach the fish (and certainly not while 'blind'), you will definitely have trouble getting the invisible fish into your net, under these conditions. Spending ten minutes repeatedly swimming a salmon round that you cannot see, within a few feet of yourself, hoping for a glimpse of it so that you can get it into the net, may be agonisingly tense, but unless you have latent masochistic tendencies you will not regard it as fun. Never mind the bitter fury of frustration if it gets off after an age of fruitless manoeuvring in the dark, while you know that in daylight it would have been into the net in a third of the time. As a rule, I am only fishing in these very dark and misty conditions because I have but a short way to go to finish off the pool before packing up for the night. The crucial decision to carry on for the extra quarter of an hour needed to properly complete the pool, rather than leave it half fished, has paid off time and again for me.

I have been amused by various articles that have recently appeared in the angling press. These have suggested that lady anglers catch far more salmon than men, and that this is because female pheromones are somehow released into the water and attract the fish to the ladies' flies. This is supported by tales of an incident in the USA where the hand of a man was dipped into a bucket of water, which was then poured into the river above a fall and this immediately appeared to cause the salmon to stop jumping. However, a woman's hand appeared to have no effect on the fish's jumping. The theory is also supported by a highly selective culling of statistics with the intent of showing that all the biggest salmon in this country have been caught by lady anglers.

It's a lovely theory. If only it were true. Us men, poor inferior mortals that we are, would never need to have an excuse for failing to catch a salmon; we could always blame our pheromones! If I wanted to be sure of catching salmon, I would just have to take a girlfriend on holiday, get her to tie on my fly, and then make her trail her fingers in the waters of the pool above. Better still, I would probably have a bonanza if I persuaded her to go in for a swim. If, in February or March, she refused, I could always throw her in anyway, to assure myself of sport!

Sadly, the theory is not worth the paper it has been written on. If it was, a single man going for a swim would immediately stop salmon being caught anywhere downstream of where he went in. At Ballogie I have caught salmon in the Inchbares, while up to 30 or 40 people have been splashing around, and swimming in the Bridge Pool and the Pot, several hundred yards upstream.

It takes more than the hand of one man or one woman to prove a theory. Proper scientific tests would have to be carried out using the hands of thousands of men and women to see if they all produced these effects, and if not what proportion did, and to identify the substances involved. I have never heard of such a trial being run. Also the salmon, in the American incident, were Pacific salmon, which, apparently, are more closely related to the rainbow trout than they are to the Atlantic salmon. Different species do not necessarily show the same reactions to a stimulus.

As for the idea of female pheromones being released from the fly, that is also subject to a lot of doubt. In order for them to reach salmon lying on the bed of the river, and across its full width, they would have to be very highly soluble. So soluble, in fact, that they would not adhere to the fly for more than a very short period, so that by the time the lady angler had progressed some way down the pool, her fly would be the same as anyone else's. Similarly, if male pheromones contain an inhibitant, a fly touched by a man would soon lose this effect after a short time. And what would happen if a male gillie tied on a lady angler's fly? Would this not confuse the salmon mightily?

As for contact between the angler's hands or body and the water, most of us do our best to avoid this. It is too cold. I do not normally touch the water at all during a day's fishing, apart from occasionally rinsing the slime from my hands after landing a fish. This does not appear to stop me from catching another a few casts later.

As for women catching all the big fish, a quick look at the lists in the late John Ashley-Cooper's book, *A Line on Salmon* shows that of the six largest salmon whose capture is officially authenticated in this country, three were caught by ladies, and three were caught by men. However, if one progresses further down the lists, one finds that the vast majority of salmon caught weighing over 50 lb were captured by men.

I do suspect that the average female angler may be better than the average male angler. This has nothing to do with pheromones, however. Lady anglers are comparatively few in number. Those that do take up the sport will probably do so because they are genuinely interested, possibly far more so than their male counterpart. They are therefore more likely to think about what they are doing, than men, who will so often fish mechanically with their minds elsewhere. They are also more likely to try to follow their gillie's instructions with care, whereas all too many men believe that they know it all already, and do not listen. Ladies are also renowned for the qualities of persistence and perseverance, which are invaluable assets to a good fisher.

However, there has not, to my knowledge, been a lady salmon fisher who possessed such genius that she dominated the sport. This is not to say that I do not know some very skilled lady anglers (and have heard of others), who cast a beautiful line, fish their flies diligently and attractively, and who have caught thousands of salmon. However, I have never heard of one who dominated sport on the rivers that she fished, in the same way that, say, Arthur Wood dominated sport on the Dee, or Robert Pashley on the Wye. These men stood, not just head and shoulders above the crowds of fellow anglers, but on pedestals beyond their reach. The giants of salmon fishing have all been men.

As far as the angler, male (or female), is concerned, the only real requirement for his sport is that there should be some salmon in the beat that he's fishing. Everything else is not essential, but adding each favourable condition in succession will progressively increase the chances of enjoying a good catch. However, it should be his ambition to understand his quarry so well that he can succeed in the worst of conditions, and not just at those times when everything is favourable.

Part 2 — Preparation

Section 1: Tackle

In preparing for any fishing trip, selecting appropriate tackle significantly affects the resulting success and enjoyment. However, attention to detail, in ensuring that all equipment is sound and well cared for, is as important, but often overlooked. The following tale illustrates the danger of neglecting maintenance.

The Willow Bush Pool lies below the island at the bottom of the Bridge Pool at Monymusk on the Don. It is situated at a right-hand bend in the river, and the current flows towards, and under, the willows on the left bank at the top, before turning across to the right, to flow in a broad sweep down through the bottom half. In low water, the fish lie in the fast stream at the top, about five yards out from the willows, and the best lie is about a third of the way down, behind a couple of rocks.

I wade down the slack water at the top of the pool, under the bank on the right-hand (south) side. This keeps me below the skyline, and so helps to conceal me from the fish. It is a typical early September day in 1979, with a blustery west wind driving scattered clouds across a sunny sky. I am fishing with my Sharpe's 13-ft cane fly rod, a floating line, and two flies, a quarter-inch Stoat's Tail Tube, and for the dropper, a quarter-inch Red and Black Tube. Because of the low water, and the small flies, the leader is tapered down to 8 lb. My trusty net, which I made as a schoolboy in metal-work classes, is slung over my shoulders.

I am casting a short line, perhaps 20 yards, more or less square across the pool, and immediately putting a large upstream mend into the line. Then, with the rod tip held high over the river allowing the flies to move downstream more slowly than the water, as the curve is straightened out of the line by the current. The line straightens at an angle of about 30° downstream, where I put in another, smaller mend before allowing the flies to fish gently round to my side of the river.

A third of the way down the pool, and just as the line is straightening in mid-stream, there is a sudden pull, and I am into a fish. This soon jumps clear of the water to reveal that it is quite fresh, and a little under eight pounds. I move back, to play the fish out, standing in the quiet water under the bank. It has taken the tail fly, and I soon have it well under control. With the rod in my left hand, and the net in my right, I lead it gently round, and slide it head first safely into the net. Turning for the bank, I lift the fish clear of the water, only to watch horrified as it falls through the mesh at the bottom of the net, and back into the river with a splash. As it does so, the dropper catches in the mesh of the net, and with a ping the leader breaks, and the fish is free.

Instantly, it wakes up to its freedom, and dashes off towards deep water. I turn, and slash the net down into the water in front of the departing fish. The rim of the net hits the bottom, and the fish avoids it with ease, altering course, but still heading out into the stream. I take a couple of rapid strides in pursuit, and again bring the net hard down into the water in front of the fish. Too hard, for the rim of the net again hits the bottom of the river, and this time the handle breaks at the ferrule joining it to the rim. The fish again avoids the net, turning to swim quickly downstream, parallel to the bank.

Dropping the rod, and the remains of the handle, I seize the rim of the net with both hands, and make a last, despairing dive headlong into the water, and onto the fleeing fish, trying to pin it to the bottom of the river with the net. Partial success, but the head and shoulders of the fish still project out from under the rim of the net, and it struggles desperately.

By now, the fish and I are in a couple of feet of water, and I am floating, beginning to drift downstream off the fish. There is a gap between the rim and the bottom of the river, and I struggle to stop the fish escaping through it. I manage to grab the shoulders of the fish through the mesh with my left hand, and then, at last, I am able to grasp the tail of the fish through the mesh with my right hand. With the head and tail of the fish firmly gripped in both hands, I struggle to my feet, and, with water pouring off me, wade back to the bank.

After killing the fish, I return to rescue my rod from the river, and then head for home, and a change of clothing. I am more than happy to have turned disaster back into triumph, even after a performance that would have graced any pantomime stage. Had the event been captured on film, it would have produced a great deal of amusement among my fishing friends, and many wry comments at my expense!

The reason that this fish was singularly unfortunate not to escape with its life was that I had neglected to check that the mesh of the net was still sound, after using it for many seasons. Sunlight degrades nylon fibres, and prolonged exposure to daylight while fishing each year had left the mesh absolutely rotten, with the inevitable consequence of failure. The moral of this tale is that one must always check one's tackle before use: all of it, and regularly.

Caring for your equipment, and taking care to obtain the right equipment, are crucial elements of salmon fishing preparation. Before buying any significant item you should think about how, where and when you will use it. In the early stages of building up a library of tackle it is sensible to avoid duplication of function. It may be wiser to choose tackle that will enable you to cope with a wider range of conditions, gradually filling in the gaps in your armoury as time goes by.

Try, always, to buy the best quality available, for it is false economy to skimp on tackle. A good fly rod or reel will last far longer than ten years if properly cared for. Even if you only fish for a dozen days each year, a rod initially priced at £250 will only have cost you a couple of pounds per day's use over ten years. You will probably have spent far more driving to and from the river each day.

Quality does not always mean paying a small fortune for expensive brand names or a fancy finish. For example, the System Two reels that I use for most of my salmon fishing currently retail at around £70–80. This is a fraction of the price of some top of the range models that I have seen. At the other end of the scale there are reels costing little more than £20, but their performance and reliability do not generally measure up to my standards. Functional requirements rather than price should dictate your choice of tackle.

Always replenish your stocks of angling consumables such as flies, nylon, treble hooks etc., before your season starts. Do not get into the habit of borrowing (!) such items from your fishing companions, who may be too polite to comment, but will recall that you made a similar request last year. Never penny pinch by rebending partly straightened hooks, or continuing to use unreliable nylon. If you do, and the fish of a lifetime's dreams escapes as a result, you will have only yourself to blame. 'Bad luck' has nothing to do with it, and it is your fault that the avoidable loss occurred.

It is also sensible to evolve a personal routine to ensure that no vital equipment is left behind. I have come to rely on checklists to avoid the risk of wasting precious hours and money trying to replace forgotten items once I have arrived at my destination. A series of checklists to cover not only the tackle you take on holiday, but also pre-season maintenance tasks, can save a lot of frustration.

Your maintenance checklist should cover the repair or replacement of items damaged, lost, destroyed or otherwise consumed during the course of the previous season's fishing. This will include everything from replacing damaged rod rings, examining and repairing waders, checking reels to see that they are properly greased and free of grit, looking at lines to see that they are not excessively worn or cracked, checking nets, restocking with appropriate hooks, nylon, flies etc., to the renewal of splices joining lines to backing, and many other small tasks. A half day or so during the winter months spent in attending to such details will definitely not have been wasted.

Make a checklist for the contents of each bag, noting, for instance, each box containing each class of fly, such as singles, doubles, trebles, plastic, aluminium and brass tubes, etc; each spool of nylon of different strength, (it is worth having these in dispensers to stop them unravelling in your bag); treble hooks of appropriate sizes, scissors, polaroid glasses, priest, thermometer, spring balance, knife, a length of stout nylon cord, etc. Also make lists of your rods, the contents of your reel bag, and clothing to be packed.

Finally, make a list of items to be packed into the car, so you can check off each one as it goes in. It might read something like this: fly rods, reel bag, fly bag, spares and repairs bag, waders and boots, net, basses (for carrying fish), insect repellent, rain top, cold weather kit, suitcase of clothing, food and drink (if self-catering), dustbin liners (for wrapping fish in if they are to be frozen), roll of paper towels (useful for everything from windscreen cleaning to emergency lavatory paper), torch, cash, cheque book, credit cards, and passport or tickets if required. All this should help to minimize the risk of any serious omission from your kit.

In the early season, it is sensible to take a spade or shovel with you in the boot of your car, either to dig yourself out of a snow-drift, or to break the ice down the side of the river, if it freezes hard.

This attention to detail in preparation is vital, and will significantly add to your enjoyment and success over the years.

Rods

Rods are vital tools with several distinct functions. During casting they act as a spring lever to catapult line and fly across the river. The ability to control the movement of line and fly at a distance is proportional to the length of the rod. In playing a fish, the rod acts both as a shock absorber to dampen the effect of sudden jerks, and as a lever to lift the line over obstacles or to manoeuvre the fish at close quarters.

Some manufacturers seem to advertise their rods solely as casting tools, which is probably unwise, since many reservoir trout fishers can cast as far with a single-handed rod, 9 or 10 feet long, as most salmon fishers can reach with a double handed 15 foot rod. However, a long rod is an essential aid in helping control the movement of the fly in the water, and at any distance over 25 yards, a short rod is simply inadequate in this respect. If you cannot cast 30 yards comfortably and consistently with a 15-ft rod, then do, please, visit a competent casting instructor. Few investments will yield such a swift and beneficial return.

A soft actioned rod may be a delight for casting and fishing the floating line, but not up to the tasks of coping with a full sunk line and 3in brass tube, or big fish in heavy water. A powerful, fast actioned rod may be just right for early spring fish on big rivers but too clumsy when a more delicate approach is needed. The heavy line it requires will create excessive disturbance in low water, and its power will rip small hooks from the soft mouths of grilse. So think how and where you intend to use a rod before making a purchase.

Nowadays rods are usually made from synthetic materials such as carbon fibre, and most are circular in cross section. However, some, such as Bruce & Walker's 'Hexagraph' range, are built from strips of carbon fibre, and a rigid central foam core, to make a hexagonal cross section, similar to the split cane rods of yesteryear. They have one big advantage over normal rods with a hollow circular cross section, and that is their superiority when it comes to playing a fish, particularly a large fish in a heavy stream, where considerable pressure may be needed. Their disadvantages are their slightly increased weight, and that some people take a while to adjust to their different casting action.

Ordinary rods have their advantages in being lighter, and that some anglers find them easier to cast with, and they are in general cheaper than the 'Hexagraph', or similar types of rod. When a rod with a circular cross-section is bent through a large angle, the cross section will tend to distort slightly, so that it becomes progressively more oval than circular, as the angle of bend is increased. This 'ovality', as it is known, is much less of a problem with the 'Hexagraph', and accounts for its better performance when it comes to playing fish. Ovality will tend to reduce the strength of a rod of circular cross-section once it has been loaded past a certain point, so that a small increase in load may lead to a large increase in the amount that the rod bends. Many rod manufacturers use a number of different methods to combat ovality, by, for example, thickening the walls of the rod blank, or using contracyclicly woven fibres to reduce the distortion.

Whatever rod I am using, I prefer it to have a screw type of reel fitting, rather than the traditional sliding ring pattern, which has to be secured with tape when in use, to prevent its working loose. To have to undo, and then replace the tape every time you swap reels on a rod, is a time-wasting bore. There are some excellent screw reel fittings, made from plastic coated alloy, which hold the reel securely, and do not need to be taped.

Always make sure the ferrules of your rod are well pushed home, and securely taped to prevent their working loose. This is essential. Never, ever try Spey casting with a rod on which the ferrules have not been taped. If an untaped joint then works loose, it will be your fault if you end up with a cracked ferrule. Check them several times a day, for signs of twisting loose, especially in hot weather. Heat will expand, and so loosen the joints. It may also reduce the adhesive performance of the glue on the tape.

For rod rings, I prefer the use of bridge rings throughout the length of the rod. With the traditional 'snake' type intermediates, I find that the line, especially if it has some memory, (i.e. retains some coils or twists after being taken off the reel), tends to rub against the rod, which will sometimes make it less easy to shoot line. Bridge rings have the virtue of keeping the line further away from the rod, although they tend to be fractionally heavier than snake rings.

Most manufacturers' rod handles are too narrow for my large, and these days, slightly arthritic hands, so now I tend to have mine made up with specially large diameter cork sections, which are easier to hold through a long day's fishing, rather than clenching my fingers around a narrow handle. The next rods that I have made up will have cork handles which are oval in section, like the shaft of an axe. These should enable me to retain a firm grip on the handle, while my hands stay fairly relaxed.

For heavy-duty sunk line work a big powerful rod is essential. I use a 16-ft 'Hexagraph' which is rated for a number 12 line. For more general sunk line fishing, I carry a slightly lighter rod of the same length, but for a number 11 line. I can also use it with a floating line, particularly when casting into a head wind. I prefer rods 15 to 17$\frac{1}{2}$-ft long, with a number 10 line, for most of my floating line fishing. The longer rod adds significantly to control at a distance over line and fly.

For smaller rivers and low water, a 12-ft rod and number 7 line is often enough, especially when the fish are not too large. I use mine when after summer grilse on the Don, and it is also light enough to use single-handed for fishing nymph or dragged surface fly techniques. However, a longer rod (15-ft) can sometimes be an advantage on small rivers, even at low water, because of the ease with which the fly can be manoeuvred around exposed rocks, or held in the right spot when dibbling at the throats of pools.

A shorter single-handed rod of about 10 feet long, casting a number 7 line, can often be used instead of the 12-ft rod, although some ability to roll and Spey cast, as well as controlling the fly at a distance, will be sacrificed. However, these disadvantages may be more than compensated by greater ease of single-handed casting and portability. Its shorter length becomes a positive advantage when casting under trees.

A rather stiff single-handed rod, equipped with a number 9 or 10 weight forward, or shooting head line, can be used for fishing the sunk fly on small rivers, where, in low water, the fish may be confined to deep pots and narrow gorges. Here very precise placing of the fly will be needed, and its accuracy, and lack of disturbance, will be major advantages. It can also be used on larger rivers to cast right across a slow-moving pool, before stripping the fly in by hand.

Reels

Choose your reels with care. They must be large enough to hold (on a big river), at least 200 yards of 30 lb braided backing, and a full 40 yards of double taper fly line. There are some who think a smaller amount of backing is adequate. They are wrong. Do not take such a foolish, and such an easily avoidable risk. On a big river, you may be fishing the tail stream of a pool, when a fish grabs your fly, turns, and goes back down the way he has just come up, heading for the next pool perhaps 200 or more yards below. If the water is at all warm, say 55°F, he will be travelling at speed, and you will not be able to stop him in the fast water between the pools. If you are wading, there may be thirty yards of boulders and pot-holes for you to scramble through, before you can reach the bank, climb out, and start to pursue your fish down the river. By the time you are ashore, the salmon, (if you are still in contact!) will be at least 150 yards below you, and you will be deeply grateful for every extra yard of line on your reel. I once lost a largish fish through not having enough line on my reel, and that certainly taught me a lesson that I do not need to have repeated.

Your reel must also have a proper disc brake, and a broad exposed rim, which is a combination that will help you maintain that steady pressure, and prevent the fish getting line too easily, which is so important to the safe management of playing a fish. Long ago I lost faith in reels with a ratchet spring check system, and I have given up using them for most of my fishing. Some disc brake systems tend to fade when they are wet, which can be a problem either when deep wading or when fishing in heavy rain. However, you can always tighten the brake in these conditions, and slacken it off again after the first couple of runs by the fish have dried things out.

Your reel must also be robust and reliable. No matter how hard you try to look after your reels, it is inevitable that they will receive a few knocks and scrapes over the years. However, most damage can be prevented with a little care. For instance, when threading the line up through the rod rings, do not put the butt of the rod, with the reel attached, on the ground, and then start threading the line through the rings, by pulling it off the reel as you go. As the spool rotates on the ground it will get scratched, and worse still, it may pick up sand or grit which could result in it jamming at a crucial moment. Instead, after attaching the reel to the butt of the rod, pull an ample quantity of line off the reel, and then place the rod butt on something, such as a seat, or a fence, or the branch of a tree, anything that will keep the reel clear of the ground while you thread the line through the rings. Very precisely engineered reels are more vulnerable to interference from sand and grit than reels machined with slightly more tolerance. However, too great a tolerance will lead to rapid, and uneven, wear of various reel parts. When not in use, keep your reels in individual pouches or cases, to protect them from knocks or picking up grit.

Lines

Over the years you will build up a range of lines to cope with different conditions and to suit your different rods. It will include everything from your lightest floating line to your heaviest ultrafast sinking shooting head. I keep mine on separate reels, as opposed to a single reel and spare spools, as a precaution against anything going wrong with the reel itself. Most of the lines should be double tapered so that they can be Spey cast.

My shooting heads have a variety of uses. They are ideal with the single-handed rod for sunk line fishing, especially on small rivers. I also like them when fishing from a boat. Providing it is kept tidy and obstruction free, the smooth floor of a boat forms a good surface on which the running line can be coiled, and there is no worry that the fly will come too close to the oars or the boatman during casting, with only the short shooting head outside the rod tip. It is easier to cast a large fly into a head wind with a shooting head than with a double taper. Where ultrafast sinking tackle is required, a shooting head is essential. The idea of trying to cast a double taper, capable of sinking 40 feet down into a pool with a heavy current, makes me shudder. On Norway's River Vosso I use a 700 grain Deep Water Express shooting head and the fly may be tied on a 3in length of

4 mm brass tube. The combination takes minimal effort to cast huge distances both neatly and safely, but sinks like a brick dropped into a mineshaft.

Although shooting heads can often be cast much further than ordinary double taper lines, they do have disadvantages, mainly associated with the light running line, which is shot through the rings with each cast. This cannot be mended satisfactorily, which reduces control over the fly in the water. Even the slickest and limpest of running lines will tangle or become snagged in bankside vegetation, which can be very frustrating. When wading, any current will drag on the running line making it difficult to shoot. The trout fisherman's line tray cannot be used when wading more than thigh deep. Stripping in 30 or 40 yards of running line by hand, prior to each cast, takes time, so that fewer casts are achieved in a day's fishing than would be possible when Spey casting the full length of a double taper line. One may be casting further with the shooting head, but actually fishing less water.

I use nylon of at least 30 lb breaking strain for my running line. Many commercial running lines are intended for use by trout fishermen, and have breaking strains of 20 lb or less. You may be using a leader that tapers down to 25 lb. If you do not ensure that your running line or backing is substantially stronger than your leader, you will be courting an expensive disaster every time your fly snags a rock in midstream, and risk losing your line as well as your fly.

My range of double tapered lines is intended to help present the fly correctly in a variety of situations. In deep or fast water a quick sinking line will be needed to fish the sunk fly attractively. Where the water is neither as deep nor as fast, a medium sinker may be better. I make mine by splicing about 20 ft of not very fast sinker (such as a Wet Cel II), to the body of a floating line from which I have removed the front tapered portion. This has advantages over a standard medium sinker which sinks throughout its length. The tip of the line will fish at the right depth while the body either floats clear of, or can be lifted over obstructions in the river, such as boulders or banks of shingle. The floating body of the line is visible, so I have a more accurate idea of the position of the fly. It is also possible to mend some of the floating body, and therefore have more control over the fishing of the fly.

Sink tip lines can be used either for fishing the sunk fly in slow or shallow water, or as a substitute for the floating line in fast gliding water, where the fly might otherwise skate on the surface.

The floating line is normally used for all methods of fishing the fly near or on the surface of the water. Sometimes it can also be used to advantage in fishing the sunk fly. In shallow water, perhaps three to five feet deep, and strewn with boulders poking through the surface, even a sink tip line would become hopelessly wrapped around the rocks with every cast. However, a 1½in or 2in brass tube fished with the floating line will sink deep enough, and with short accurate casts, the long rod can lift and manoeuvre the line over or around obstacles to deadly effect.

Although midwater presentation (with the fly one or two feet down), does not usually work as well as the fully sunk, or the fly fished near the surface, it sometimes succeeds when all else fails. A floating, or intermediate line, often with a slightly larger than usual fly, is generally used for this presentation.

Leaders

A tapered leader helps turn the fly over correctly, so that it falls neatly beyond the end of the line during casting. I usually make mine up from spools of different strength nylon. I begin by needle knotting a length of 35 lb nylon to the end of the fly line, and then adding a series of progressively finer pieces to give me a leader of the required length and tip strength.

For the floating line, I usually fish with a leader 15–17 ft long, and tapered down to 12 or 15 lb. For most sunk line fishing I use a leader about 8 ft long, tapering down to 18 or 20 lb. For very heavy flies, or the big water and big fish conditions one experiences in Norway, a finest section of 25 lb may be more sensible. I sometimes use a longer leader (over 12 ft) with the sunk line. This is for low-water fishing when I may have to do a lot of hand-lining with relatively small flies. It improves presentation by allowing the fly to sink more deeply into the water, as well as increasing the separation between it and the end of the line. When hand-lining, the line may pass over the fish before it sees the fly, unlike most forms of presentation, where the object is to show the lure to the fish first.

For low water on smaller rivers without too many rocks, or when using very small flies or certain presentation styles, such as the nymph, or a little dragged surface fly, I may use finer nylon, as light as 8lb. For larger, or rocky rivers, I do not like to go below about 10 or 12lb.

I use a needle knot to attach the butt to the fly line because it is neat, strong, and will not become stuck in the tip ring if I reel in too far while playing a fish. Also a needle knot does not cause a wake on the surface when fishing gliding water with the floating line. Loop to loop, or loop to figure-of-eight knots are less satisfactory in these areas, although scoring in convenience.

Leaders made from braided nylon have appeared in recent years, but I am not keen on them for general salmon fishing, although they will suffice for grilse and sea trout. While they improve leader turnover during casting, and are joined very neatly to the fly line by the compression caused by a tubular plastic collar, they have some disadvantages. Casting can cause the braid to wear at the end of the fly line. The ones that I tested over one and a half years were not strong enough, and I had to cut away the bottom 3 or 4 ft of a 7-ft braided leader before I could attach a tippet section of normal strength for fishing the sunk fly. Because of their rough surface, I found them difficult to knot neatly, or to tighten evenly, and the recommended water knot is much bulkier than I like.

Super, or double-strength nylons are another recent development. These are usually resin reinforced polymer cofilaments, and very much stronger in relation to their diameter than ordinary nylon. This can be an advantage when fishing with the small fly and floating line. However, great care is needed in tying knots correctly, tightening them cautiously, and watching for the slightest sign of abrasion. Double-strength nylons appear to be especially vulnerable to these problems, and at any sign of stress, the length should be discarded at once.

Match your leader and fly size. The larger the fly, the thicker the leader. Small flies need fine leaders to enable them to move around attractively in the current. Large flies need strong leaders to withstand the stress of casting, but their movement in the water will be less affected by the thickness of the nylon.

It is an affectation to fish too light a leader. It is not 'more sporting', nor does it 'give the fish a chance', other than of swimming away exhausted, with a hook stuck in its throat. So treat the beautiful, noble salmon with respect, and use a leader of sufficient strength.

I do not like leaders that fluoresce in bright sunlight. If I can see them, so can the fish. I prefer my nylon to be as transparent as possible, to lessen the risk of the fish noticing it, and turning away at the last second.

Lastly, never leave unwanted nylon on the river bank, where it can cause prolonged suffering to wild birds and animals if they become entangled. Take it home with you, together with any left by others. If that is not possible, wrap it into a ball round your fingers, and snip it into lengths of less than 2in, which will make its environmental impact minimal.

The fly

Although I was brought up in an era when the traditional patterns of salmon fly reigned supreme, for the vast bulk of my salmon fly fishing I now use only two patterns.

For my floating line I use something that I call a Hairy Mary tube, and for the sunk line I use a Drowned Mouse.

The Hairy Mary only bears a vague likeness to the standard dressing. I suspect that a fly-tying purist would probably describe it as a squirrel tail variant, or something equally tedious. Anyway, whatever its name, I thought it looked approximately like a Hairy Mary as I remembered seeing one in a friend's box, when I first tied it in 1972. It has caught me, and my friends, a lot of salmon over the years. So many, in fact, that I am happy to use it as my only fly over an entire season for all my floating line work. Its dressing is as follows:

Tag   Four turns oval silver twist tinsel
Rib   Oval silver twist tinsel
Body   Black floss

> Wing   Mixed natural black squirrel tail and dyed blue squirrel tail, tied
> all round.

The fly should be fairly lightly dressed.

If tied as a tube fly, the squirrel tail fibres should be more than long enough to cover the treble hook as well as the tube itself. Thus a fly tied on a slim $1/2$in plastic tube should have hairs approximately $1^1/4$in long. I tie it in a range of sizes, from a $1/4$in tube with an overall length of just under $3/4$in, to a $1^1/2$in tube with an overall length of just over $2^1/2$in. Even smaller flies can be made by tying a pinch of blue and black squirrel tail hairs direct to the shank of an ordinary small black outpoint treble hook. There is no need to buy specially long shanked trebles, and one can often omit the body from the dressing.

The Drowned Mouse started life as my attempt to copy a Willie Gunn that a friend was using one early season day on the Dee in 1984. However, I had noticed that as soon as a brass tube fly moved into slacker water, its body hung down at a steep angle beneath its wing, which still streamed out horizontally in the current. This often coincided with a number of abortive plucks and pulls at the fly, as it moved into slower water. What I suspected was happening, was that any fish that nipped at the head or wing of the fly, as opposed to full-bloodedly engulfing the whole thing, was not actually taking the hooks into its mouth. Something was needed to stabilise the body of the fly, to help it stay more horizontal in the water. I decided that a long tail would provide the necessary drag at the rear of the fly to create the lift needed, and so, to my existing imitation of a Willie Gunn, I added a long tail of red buck tail hair. These days, I might also suggest that I should have started to hand-line in the fly sooner, before it actually reached the slacker water, but that is by the by. Anyway, the fly was born by the spring of 1985, but it was not till May of the following year, when I was successful in very high water on the Dee, that it became established as my number one sunk fly. I originally referred to it as a 'Red, yellow, orange and black tube fly', but this was too long and clumsy to be a good name, and a 'Willie Gunn with a long red tail' was not satisfactory either. However, it was Gylla Lawrence, who, after looking at my catch on the 8 May 1986, and asking what I had caught them on, announced that 'It looks like a drowned mouse to me', and the name stuck. Here is the dressing:

> Tail   Red Bucktail
> Butt   Four or five turns oval silver twist tinsel
> Rib   Oval silver twist tinsel
> Body   Black floss
> Wing   Yellow bucktail, tied underneath orange bucktail, tied underneath
> black bucktail

Both the tail, and all parts of the wing are tied all the way round the tube, and both should overlap the end of the tube to more than cover the treble, so that a 2in tube implies a fly with an overall length of about 4in. A 3in tube means a fly with an overall length of over 5in.

Most of the flies are tied on brass tubes, in a range of sizes from 1in to 3in. I also tie a few on aluminium and plastic tubes, and a few on extra heavy brass tubes for work in very high and fast water.

Why such a limited selection of patterns? Because I do not think that the pattern matters that much to the fish. For floating line fishing, all that the fish often sees of the fly, before launching itself up from the bottom, is a small dark silhouette against the surface of the water. Stick a fly on a window pane, and look up at it silhouetted against a bright sky, from a distance of about seven feet. Sometimes, when looking at a fly in this way, one cannot even tell what colour it is, never mind picking out intricate details of pattern. The salmon, lying in several feet of water, only has a few seconds in which to make up its mind before the fly moves out of its field of vision, and so whether the fly has bars or stars probably will not make much difference. However, whether the fly moves in a lifelike manner is much more apparent to the fish. In the chapter on presentation, I discuss the size of the fly, and its movement relative to the water and to the fish, and the effect of the temperature of the water on this relationship. All these factors are much more important than the pattern of the fly, so that the way you fish a fly will largely determine whether it is a successful pattern or not.

With the sunk fly, the salmon is likely to be much closer to the lure, and therefore to see it in more detail, before moving in to attack. Indeed, in very cold water your fly may need to pass within a foot of the nose of the salmon to trigger a feeding response. However, I normally use only one pattern of sunk fly for very practical reasons, and concentrate on presenting it correctly.

I would otherwise waste too much time in deciding whether my fly should contrast or blend in with the background of water and river bed, or to change it in bright sunlight or overcast conditions, or what to do when salmon lie over bright shingle and dark rock in the same pool.

So I stick to the Drowned Mouse. The red, yellow and orange of its tail and wing shows up well against a dark background, but they are partially masked by the black of the top layer of the wing, which, when combined with the black body, makes the fly show dark against a light background. The silver rib helps to break up the straight outline of the body, and also adds a little sparkle, which might make the fly more easily seen in some conditions. Thus it seems to satisfy the criteria needed for a good, general purpose sunk fly, being neither too bright nor over dull.

Whatever pattern you finally settle on as your main sunk fly, do make sure that you have enough dressed in each size. You will need at least three or four, and preferably half a dozen copies in each size. During the course of a week or two's fishing, it is inevitable that the dressing on some flies will become damaged, and that others may be lost among the rocks of the river bed, so always start with enough spares to see you through the week. Remember, you might arrive to find the water very low, and you fish all week without using anything heavier than a $1^{1}/_{2}$in brass tube. Or, you find the river running bank high with melting snow and need a 3in brass tube all week. So it is wise not to skimp on the numbers of flies that you have at the very small, or very large ends of the range.

Years ago, when I still used my spinning rod regularly, I never managed to prove to myself that there was any consistent gain in switching from a Brown & Gold Devon to a Black & Gold, or to a Yellow Belly, so I would use the same one all day. Equally I could never prove that changing the pattern of fly made any consistent difference. However, changes in the depth and speed at which either lure was fished were crucial to success.

Using only one pattern saves time that otherwise would be wasted changing flies, and frees one from the weight of the extra boxes that would have to be carried to provide a full range of different sizes in different patterns. It also prevents me worrying about whether I am using the right pattern or not, something that might otherwise unsettle concentration and confidence.

I have seldom read a convincing account of the superiority of one established pattern over another. Almost invariably, the evidence is circumstantial, and there is a distinct lack of scientific proof. For example, a typical account would describe an angler fishing unsuccessfully all morning with, say, a Yellow Dog tube fly. In the afternoon he switches to a Purple Prawn fly, fishes the same pools again, and catches several fish. The conclusion is that the only fly to interest the fish that day was a Purple Prawn.

However, the case is not proven, because the different response of the fish in the morning and afternoon could have been due to, say, a small change in environmental conditions such as water height, temperature, or degree of acidity. Or a group of fresh fish might have arrived during the afternoon. The flies might have been of different sizes, or weights or thickness of dressing so that one was fished incorrectly in the morning but the other was fished correctly in the afternoon. The list of possible reasons is almost endless, and it is unwise to jump to a conclusion that one pattern is better than another on such tenuous evidence.

There may be rare occasions when a salmon will respond to a purple fly and not to a yellow fly when both are correctly presented. However, the fisherman does not know this in advance, and finding out is likely to take a very long time, which could be more productively spent elsewhere. He may change his yellow fly to a black one, to an orange one, to a green one, to a red one, to a brown one to a silvery one and so on, without ever finding the right one.

It is far better to concentrate on presenting your fly correctly. If you have only one pattern in your box, you only have to decide what size to use, and how to fish it. A multiplicity of patterns is an avoidable complication.

I do have a handful of specials for occasional use. Some are described by my friends as 'Christmas tree decorations', because, with a mylar body and wings of gold and silver lurex mixed with yellow and orange hair, they are very bright. I use them for fishing muddy waters in spate conditions when there is an obvious premium in making the fly as visible as possible. Other hairy monsters are tied for my own amusement and no other reason. I fish them for the fun of it.

However, for at least 90 per cent of my fishing I use only one pattern for the floating line, and one for the sunk line, but I would happily use the Drowned Mouse for both methods.

Arthur Wood used to catch several hundred salmon in a typical season, far more than many of today's anglers do in their entire lives. Although he normally fished with two patterns (a Blue Charm or a Silver Blue) he was happy to use just a March Brown throughout the season. You could do far worse than follow his example.

Section 2: Clothing

A good angler should not be caught unprepared by the weather, no matter how unseasonal, or rapid the fluctuations between one extreme and the other. On the Aberdeenshire Dee, at around the end of April and beginning of May, I have grown used to temperatures fluctuating by as much as 50°F in the space of three or four days. That means temperatures falling from over 80°F and heatwave conditions, to overnight frost and snow, with daytime temperatures in the middle to upper 30sF. During the same period, water temperatures may fall by 25°F. Such abrupt changes are not unusual, and it is only common sense to be prepared for all eventualities. It is foolish to travel up to Scotland for a week's salmon fishing in the spring, and not to bring the appropriate cold and wet weather kit, just because there has been a fortnight's hot and sunny weather. However, at the same time you should not forget to bring a tube of the appropriate lotion needed to protect you from the sun.

A proper range of protective clothing is an essential part of preparation, and a sound investment. It can also be worn for activities other than just salmon fishing, so it is unlikely to remain under used. If you can stay comfortably warm and dry in the worst of weather conditions, you can continue to concentrate on your fishing. If you are cold, wet and miserable, you will not be able to concentrate satisfactorily, and your chances of success will suffer accordingly.

My list of clothing for early season fishing has been built up over the years.

Hard sole chest waders	1 pair
Soft-sole chest wader	1 pair
Felt soled boots for soft soled chest waders	1 pair
Thigh waders	1 pair
Cold weather jacket	1
Rain top jackets	2
Thermal pile trousers	2 pairs
Thermal pile jacket	2
Wading socks	3 pairs
Thick woollen stockings	6 pairs
Lined leather gloves	2 pairs
Fingerless mitt	2 pairs
Palmless mitts (sheepskin)	2 pairs
Scarves (wool or cotton towelling)	2
Hat	1
Woollen sweaters (heavy)	3
Woollen sweaters (light)	2
Shirts (heavy cotton, brushed cotton, wool and cotton)	
Trousers (Tweed, or heavy corduroy, or moleskin, etc.)	
Underclothes, handkerchiefs etc.	

Whenever you are fishing away from home, always keep a bag containing a complete change of clothing in the car, in case you fall in, or suffer some similar disaster.

It may help to consider, briefly, some of the items on my list.

Waders

Hard-sole waders are easy to pull on and off. However, they offer little to protect your feet from rocks, and little to support your ankles. They also tend to be made too short in the leg, which reduces your freedom of movement, and makes it difficult to climb over rocks in the river, or over fences and stiles, or up steep banks. They are therefore not the most comfortable things to wear for walking long distances, but they are adequate for use where the wading, walking and river banks are not too demanding.

Soft-sole waders are more of a bother to put on, and to take off, as they require a separate pair of boots. However, these boots will provide better protection for your feet, and support for your ankles. Soft-sole waders also tend to be better cut, with longer legs offering greater freedom of movement. Their slimmer profile, combined with the stronger boot, means that they are more suited to wading where there is a fast current or a rocky bottom or the two combined. They are also more comfortable to walk in. At the moment I use some made from 4 mm closed cell neoprene rubber, which has good insulating properties, is resistant to abrasion, and, because of its elasticity, is very flexible. They are the best waders that I have found so far. They also have the virtue of being positively buoyant in the water.

It is always sensible to have more than one pair of waders available when you are fishing. Aside from anything else, waders get very sweaty when used continuously, and it is nice to be able to alternate between pairs, so that each has a chance to dry out while the other is being used. Always hang your waders up when not in use, so that the air can circulate to dry them. Soft-sole waders can be hung up inside out, so that the interior dries properly. Having more than one pair of waders available helps to avoid disaster if you sit on a briar, or trip over a piece of barbed wire concealed by the grass on the bank. You can carry on fishing in your spare pair of waders, and repair the punctured ones at your leisure.

Thigh waders are for paddling in, not for wading rivers like the Dee or the Spey. I use mine either for splashing about on small rivers, or for use on large rivers in near spate conditions, when I have no intention of wading. For instance, I may be fishing the Dee when it is running bank high with melting snow, and the only time that I intend to set foot even half into the river, is to land a fish. There is little point in my lumbering around in the heat, in a pair of chest waders, if I can avoid it.

Considering the importance of a sure footing on the bed of a river, it is sad that waders have seen so little improvement in the design of their soles in recent years. Felt soles were certainly in use by the 1920s, and may even have been used before then. One French manufacturer has made a step in the right direction, by mixing fibres of steel wool in a synthetic rubber to make a sole for his boots, but the result is by no means perfect, and further progress must be made. Felt soles do provide a little grip on smooth and slippery rocks. However, they do not provide any grip on slimy, algae coated rocks, nor on wet grass, mud, clay or chalk. This means that there is always the possibility of a crashing fall on a steep bank. To reduce the possibility of such a sudden fall, the best available combination at the moment is probably a studded felt sole and a hard, studded heel. Felt soles also build up lumps of snow, sometimes several inches thick, when the angler is fishing on the bank in snowy weather. This obviously increases the risk of a fall or a twisted ankle.

I hope that someone will develop a sole made from small, close-set tufts of steel wires deeply fixed in rubber or plastic. This might have the flexibility of surface needed to cope with smooth rocks, and the abrasiveness to cut through slime, and to get a grip on clay bottoms, or wet grass and muddy banks.

In the top pocket of my chest waders, I carry a thermometer and a priest.

Cold weather jacket and rain tops

I use my cold weather jacket for fishing in blizzard conditions, or other equally unpleasant early season weather. My cold weather jacket consists of a Gore-Tex outer shell and a quilted Thinsulate lining. It has a storm front and cuffs, a high collar, and a properly designed, insulated hood with a wired peak. In stormy weather, the drawstring on the hood can be done up tightly, so that there is a slit for the mouth, and only the eyes and nose are left uncovered. If polaroid spectacles are worn, and the wired peak is correctly adjusted, almost all your face will be covered, and protected from snow, and hailstones. I wear this jacket inside my chest waders.

I wear a rain top outside my chest waders to ensure that that is where the rain and snow runs off, and not into my waders. It is a short jacket made of unlined Gore-Tex with a storm front and cuffs, and an integral hood with a wired peak. There are some plastic jackets available at a fraction of the price, but these tend to have problems with perspiration and condensation, which can reduce the insulation of other clothing.

Another advantage of wearing your rain top properly done up, outside your waders, is that if you trip, fall in, and rapidly scramble to your feet, you may well get away without shipping any water at all, or only a little. This is definitely more attractive than the several gallons of often icy water that will probably find their way into your waders, if you sit down in the river when not wearing a properly done up rain top. The combination of cold weather jacket inside, and rain top outside your chest waders will result in so much air being trapped inside your clothing that you will be positively buoyant, and can scramble out, not much the worse for wear, even if you have been washed some distance downstream.

The rain top should be short, not hanging below your crutch, so that it does not increase the drag of the current.

In bad weather, a properly designed hood is essential. Some manufacturers treat hoods as optional extras, which is wrong, and irresponsibly so. A well constructed hood is far superior to any combination of hat and scarves in preventing heat loss from head and neck.

I remember fishing with my friend Malcolm Hay on a cold March day at Monymusk. A squally shower of hail and snow, driven by a near gale force northerly wind, had continued unabated while we enjoyed our lunch in the house. It was still blizzarding when we emerged, with an inch or two of snow and hail already on the ground, but fortunately the first pool was sheltered from the north by a small wood. After this we crossed over the river to fish on down with the wind behind us from the north bank.

With no sign of the storm lessening, I was glad to have my back to the icy blast, and not to have to face into the horizontally driven hailstones. The blizzard only started to clear when we reached the bottom pool, Anne's Seat. Malcolm was fishing this down with a spinner, and I followed about sixty yards behind him with the fly. He began to complain about the cold, and when I reached him, I saw why. He was wearing a waterproof coat, and a tweed cap. There was a gap of three or four inches between the top of his turned up collar and the bottom of his cap. Here the hail and snow had stuck to his hair, and had built up into lumps of ice the size of oranges. No wonder he was cold! By contrast, my hood had provided my head and neck with more than adequate protection, and I was still warm, dry and comfortable. As we trudged back through the snow and hail that was now lying several inches deep, the weather cleared completely, and we reached the house in brilliant sunshine. Poor Malcolm took about two or three hours to thaw out in front of the fire before he felt restored enough to drive home.

This shows the advantage of a hood over a hat in terms of bad weather protection. To this day, my conscience still troubles me occasionally over my thoughtlessness in not noticing Malcolm's plight sooner.

While you are holding your rod in the rain, water will run down the outside of your sleeves and onto your hands. When you raise them during casting, it will try to run down your arms inside your sleeves. Storm cuffs act as a barrier to help reduce this. On a day of continuous heavy rain, I will sometimes wear two rain tops at the same time, one inside, and one outside my chest waders. Thus protected, I stay dry in the worst of downpours, having two sets of seals to prevent leaks around the face and cuffs, and extra protection to prevent water getting through at stretch points, such as elbows and shoulders.

Mountaineering, sailing and motorcycle shops understand the importance of proper protective clothing far more than many fishing shops. Modern 'breathable' waterproof clothing fabrics such as Gore-Tex are vastly superior to waxed cotton, which only stays waterproof if it is rewaxed after every two weeks of wear. Waxed cotton is also heavy, and unpleasantly hot to walk in if the weather is warm. If kept properly waxed, this rubs off onto car seats, collecting dirt, and transferring itself to the clothing of any smartly dressed person who occupies the seat in the future. As a piece of First World War technology, it should only be of historic interest to the serious modern salmon fisher.

Thermal pile trousers and jackets
Thermal pile fabrics are made from synthetic fibres such as nylon or dacron, woven to give a cloth with a thick, soft, fleecy pile, which provides good insulation, and also helps to draw perspiration away from the body. Jackets and trousers made from these fabrics are good value, being both warm and relatively cheap. However, to be effective, they must be worn under windproof outer garments. The trousers are excellent insulation for your legs when worn inside a pair of chest waders. Wear them on top of your ordinary trousers. I wear the jacket under a rain top in cold weather, when conditions are not extreme enough to warrant the use of the cold weather jacket. I keep a spare set in my bag containing an emergency change of clothing.

Thick wool wading socks and stockings
I always take at least three pairs of wading socks with me, keeping one in my bag, and use the other two alternately so that I always have a dry pair to put on each day. In very cold water I have pairs with special Thinsulate linings, which offer even better insulation. Wearing a fresh pair of woollen stockings every day stops them getting damp with perspiration, and therefore improves their insulating qualities.

Lined leather gloves, fingerless mitts, and palmless mitts
Having two pairs of each means that I can keep spares in my emergency bag, so that if one set becomes soaked by the rain, or if I dip a hand in the river, (which is easily done while wading waist deep), I always have dry replacements available. Having such a collection, I can perm the different combinations to suit my exact requirements depending on the severity of the weather. For instance, in cold wet weather, I will wear a lined leather glove with a palmless mitt on top of it, on my left hand. Palmless mitts consist of a long thick knitted cuff, and a sheepskin cover for the back of the hand, which is kept in place by elasticated loops around fingers and thumb. The knitted cuff is important in reducing heat loss through the wrist. When worn on top of an ordinary lined leather glove, it dramatically improves the glove's insulating powers. The storm cuffs of cold weather jackets, and rain tops, should be done up outside (over the top of) the cuff of the palmless mitt.

On my right hand I wear a palmless mitt on top of a fingerless mitt. This combination provides as much insulation as possible to the wrist and back of my hand, while leaving the ends of my fingers and thumb uncovered for sensitivity. This is important for knotting flies to leaders, and releasing line at the correct moment in the cast, for it to be shot across the pool. In less severe weather, I can obviously discard one or both layers of glove to keep my hands comfortable.

Scarf and hat

The scarf has three functions. The first is to insulate the neck, and secondly to act as seal to prevent warm air being squeezed out from the body of your jacket every time you move your arms, as you will when casting. The third is to absorb water. In very wet and windy weather, rain that strikes your face will work its way under the seals of your hood and down your neck. Your shirt collar, and then your shirt front will gradually get wet. A scarf prevents this, and so adds materially to comfort.

I like my scarves to be soft, so that they do not irritate my neck and the underside of my chin. I prefer them to be made from cashmere, or a strip of soft cotton towelling about 4½ ft long and about 8in wide. This leave the ends long enough to be properly tucked away, and to stay in place, after the scarf has been wrapped around my neck one and three-quarters times.

I wear a hat, sometimes, when the weather is bright and blustery, but conditions are not bad enough to warrant the use of a hood. It is an old, shapeless, felt trilby, secured under my chin with a couple of bits of cord. The brim covers my ears, and also prevents sunlight from reflecting off the back of my polaroid glasses.

Selecting correctly designed and constructed clothing is as important to successful salmon fishing as choosing rods and reels. It is a vital aspect of preparation, and one that is too often neglected. Sheltering inside the hut from the cold and wet outside is the reason why many anglers catch fewer salmon than they might. It is not an excuse. With proper clothing they could be out, enjoying themselves, in the worst of conditions.

Section 3: The Approach

Reconnaissance

Local knowledge is vital. The more you know about the beat that you are fishing, the better your chances of success. Over the years you will build up a knowledge of what happens, and how the fish behave in different conditions. It starts with simple things, such as which pool is sheltered from the cruel north-east wind, or which pools are shaded by trees, so that the sun does not shine straight down the water dazzling the fish; or where a hill blocks the setting sun, so that you can start fishing there first in the evening, while other pools are still bathed in sunlight.

It progresses to a knowledge of which pools fish best at different heights of the water, and of some of the tactics you will need to employ to present your fly attractively at some of the lies.

As the years go by, you will find out things such as where, in spate conditions, you can catch salmon on the big sunk fly within a yard of the bank, as they slip upstream sheltered from the full force of the current; or where, in low water, there is a small hole in a shallow run between the pools, that sometimes holds a briefly resting fish.

You will find out precisely where you need to stand in the river, to hang your fly properly in some difficult pockets of water, and how to wade the various pools in safety at different water heights. You will learn which pools need to be fished down twice, once with the short line, and once with the long line, or where other special tactics are needed.

In time you will get to know the main routes that the fish follow, as they swim between, and through, the pools, at different heights of the water. You will have seen how flood waters can ruin the best pool on the beat by filling it with thousands of tons of shingle, or scoop out new holding pools elsewhere. You will have seen how the position, and direction of the main current flowing into, through, or out of a pool can change from year to year, and how this affects the way that the pool fishes, and the stock of fish that it will hold.

You will have learned which obstacles the fish are reluctant to ascend below a certain water temperature, and also where they pause briefly in a few square yards of water after they have swum up a rapid.

Over the years you will have gained an understanding of the beat, and the way the fish are likely to behave as they move through it. This specialist knowledge will give you a growing advantage in exploiting the potential of the water. As time goes by, the gaps in your knowledge will become fewer, but still there will always be more to find out, as the river changes from year to year, and the salmon themselves continue to surprise you.

If you fish a beat for only one week of each season, it will usually take the best part of ten years to gain any real depth of knowledge of how the beat works. If you are fortunate enough to fish it for a fortnight each year, the length of time needed will be shortened substantially. You will never gain this knowledge if you continually switch from river to river, and from beat to beat. If you find a stretch of water that you like, stick to it, and over the years you will be rewarded.

Local knowledge is so important in achieving consistent success in fishing for salmon, that it makes good sense to try to shorten the time needed to acquire it. This takes a certain amount of self-discipline, but the right approach to studying the water will help you enormously. Time spent on reconnaissance is never time wasted. People who live in the same locality as their salmon fishing have a big advantage over those who do not. They will have many more opportunities to study the water in varying conditions throughout the season.

If you do not live locally, then it is a good idea to study the water before you start fishing. Instead of arriving in time for supper on, say, Sunday evening, if your week's fishing starts on Monday morning, try to time your journey so that you will arrive at lunch-time on Sunday. Have lunch, and then set out to walk the beat, from one end to the other, and then back again. Aside from anything else, this is a good way of de-stressing yourself, and relaxing after your journey. But this is no casual stroll along the riverside.

When you begin your walk, plant a stick at the water's edge so that you can note whether the river has risen or fallen on your return. Many rivers have a regular pattern of fluctuations in level at certain times, and the height of the river will be a major influence on which order you choose to fish the pools. On a snow-fed river it may take the water from the melting snow twelve hours or twenty-four hours to reach different points in the river. Peak water volume from the day's melting snow may occur at midnight on a beat fairly high up the river, at 6 a.m. next morning on a beat in the middle reaches, and not till lunch-time or even later on beats still lower down the river. Some rivers, where the headwaters are used for hydro-electricity generation, will also have regular daily fluctuations in level, depending on the amount of generating being done. Rain-fed rivers will also tend to follow a pattern as they subside after a spate. So always plant that stick, not just on your reconnaissance trip, but every day when you are fishing. It helps to attune your mind to the river.

It would be too easy to simply say, 'Look carefully at the river as you walk along', or 'Study the characteristics of each pool'. Unfortunately for many people such general advice would be wasted, as they are simply not observant enough, unless forced to concentrate on noting the details of each piece of water. So, to make yourself pay more attention to the river, take a small notebook and a pencil with you, and try to sketch the characteristics of each section of the river.

I am not suggesting that you try to emulate Leonardo da Vinci, with a diagram of mathematical exactitude and a wealth of detail. However, a brief sketch that tries to get the line of each bank right, detailing any bend or curve, and any point that juts out, or any bay that cuts into the bank, will be more than enough to make you start looking at the river properly. Mark your sketch with circles and crosses for rocks that stick out of the water, or are covered by it, and ovals to mark the area of turbulence behind submerged rocks that could mark possible salmon lies. Draw carefully the path and extent of the current as it flows through the pool, noting areas of slack water and fast streams, and some approximations of depth.

Each sketch should take perhaps five, or at the most ten minutes to complete, and trying to get it down on paper will force you to think about what you are looking at. Before you try to draw it, you may think of a stretch of gliding water as being fairly featureless, with a broad, even current flowing down parallel to the bank through the whole pool. When you come to draw it, you may notice some boulders near the top of the pool, below which the current slopes in towards the bank on which you are standing, leaving an area of slack water behind the rocks. The current then runs more slowly, and parallel to the bank for 30 yards, before speeding up, and turning to flow diagonally away from the bank some distance above the tail of the pool. This will make a big difference to your tactics.

If you have fished the stretch before, you will know the names of the pools already. If not, you should have received a copy of a map with your lease, if it is private water, or with your permit if it is hotel or Association water. Use this map to name or number your sketches. Have a good look at the water between the pools, and do a quick sketch of areas that look 'interesting', or that might be fishable at a different water height.

Once you reach the far end of the beat, turn round and walk back. As you come to each pool, take a fresh look at the relevant little sketch, and at the water. Your different perspective may mean that your eye is drawn to various details that you had not previously noticed, and again this may help you in the future.

By the time you get back to your hotel, or wherever you are staying, you will already know the location of the most attractive looking pools on the beat at the present water height, and have a good idea of the tactics that you will use when you first fish them. For instance, if you intend to fish the sunk fly, you may have decided that a sink tip will be necessary in pool number 1, but pool number 3 requires the full fast sinking line.

If you have previously fished the beat, you will also have noted any major changes since the last time you were there, and will be thinking about how to adjust your approach to the pools concerned.

Your reconnaissance of the water will also have revealed details, such as suitable places for beaching fish; snags, such as sunken trees, to be avoided, and any pools where it is best to keep back from the edge of the bank to avoid disturbing fish lying close in. You may also have seen a few fish jumping, which will give an indication of the present stock in the beat. In addition, you will know the orientation of the pools in relation to the sun, which will help decide the times of day to fish them.

By spending several hours examining the beat carefully, you will have set your mind on the right track in thinking, both consciously and subconsciously, about the characteristics of each pool, and the tactics to employ. This will give you more than a head start over those that do not carry out a proper reconnaissance. Having looked carefully, and had time to think in depth about what you saw before starting to fish, your approach will be more positive. You will be able to decide more quickly about what tactics to use, and you will be more likely to decide correctly.

A half day's detailed reconnaissance can be worth as much as several days' fishing without it, in terms of building a store of local knowledge. Julius Caesar quite clearly understood the importance of reconnaissance, when he said *'Veni, vidi, vici';* ('I came, I saw, I conquered').

Reading and exploiting the water

Having been allocated your beat for the day, you then have to decide which sections to fish, and in which order to fish them. Your basic reconnaissance of the river should have revealed the main characteristics of each of the pools. To this information you should add:

1 The temperature of the water. This is important because, for example, some pools are much easier to fish effectively with the floating line than with the sunk line, and so may offer a better chance as the water warms in the afternoon. Also, the warmer the water, the more likely that salmon will be found in faster and shallower stretches.
2 The likely fluctuations in water level through the day. If the water level is at 3ft on the gauge at 9 a.m., and it is expected to fall to 2ft 4in by mid-afternoon, it will pay to fish the pools that are best in the higher water first.
3 The probable pattern of wind strength and direction. This is important because of its effect on casting, and controlling the fly. For instance, you might be fishing when there is an area of high pressure locked over northern Britain. The mornings are likely to be calm, but by two or three in the afternoon, there may be a stiff south-easterly breeze blowing, strong enough to trouble your casting. It is therefore sensible to try to fish the pools that will be adversely exposed to this wind in the calm of the morning, and to leave the pools that are not so affected till the afternoon.
4. The sun, and where it is in relation to various pools at different times of the day. A bright sun shining straight down the river will certainly not improve your chances with the floating line, although it has less impact on the success of the sunk line. So plan to fish the pools when the sun is shining across, rather than down them. In periods of bright sun and low water, you should also plan to make use of any times when certain pools are shaded by high banks or tall trees.

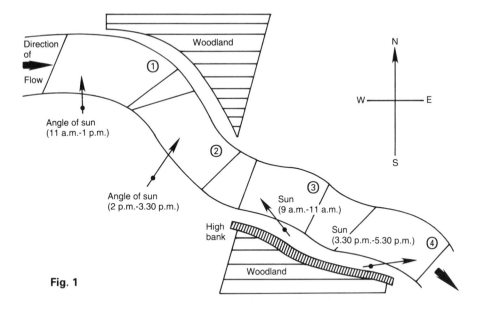

Direction of Flow

Woodland

Angle of sun
(11 a.m.-1 p.m.)

①

②

③

④

Angle of sun
(2 p.m.-3.30 p.m.)

Sun
(9 a.m.-11 a.m.)

High bank

Sun
(3.30 p.m.-5.30 p.m.)

Woodland

N

W ——————— E

S

Fig. 1

To illustrate this need to plan the order in which you fish the pools look at Fig. 1. This shows a section of a theoretical river which flows approximately from north-west to south-east. There are four main pools, and you are fishing the beat from the south bank.

Pool 1 fishes best at a height of about 2ft 8in
Pool 2 fishes best at a height of about 2ft 5in
Pool 3 fishes best at heights of over 3ft
Pool 4 fishes best at about 2ft 4in

At 9 a.m., the river is at 3ft on the gauge, and is expected to fall to about 2ft 4in by mid-afternoon.

Start off by fishing pool 3, which will be wasted if you leave it till later in the day, as there may be insufficient flow to show your fly attractively, or not enough depth to hold salmon in the lies. Also, the sun will be shining diagonally upstream, during the morning, which is ideal, if you happen to be fishing the floating line.

Next, move up to pool 1 at the top of the beat. The time will now be about 11 am, and the river will have fallen to about 2ft 8in or 2ft 9in. Fish this pool till, say, half past twelve or one o'clock, when you stop to spend half an hour eating your sandwiches. During the middle of the day, the sun will be shining straight across this pool.

After your lunch, if the river has dropped enough, move down to pool 2, if not, it might be worth giving the best bits of pool 1 a final try before you start to fish pool 2. During the early afternoon, the sun will be shining diagonally up pool 2, and in late afternoon, straight across it. In either case, this is fine.

In mid to late afternoon, move down to pool 4. The river by now will have dropped to near its lowest level of the day, at around 2ft 4in, and this pool should be fishing well. There is a high bank, with a wood growing on the top of it which shades the water from the afternoon sun, which might otherwise have been less than helpful.

If you had simply started at the top of the beat, at pool 1 and fished down from there, you would have significantly reduced your chances of success. Pools 1 and 2 would have been too high, and pool 3 would have been too low. You would have wasted much of the beat's potential.

The worst wind direction for the beat is from the north-east, but there is partial shelter from it for pools 1 and 2 due to the wood on the north bank. In a nasty northeasterly you might choose to spend more time, during that period when the wind is strongest, at pools 1 and 2. Similarly, in a south-westerly gale, which makes casting the fly very easy, but controlling it in the water very difficult, you might prefer to concentrate on pools 3 or 4 where there is some shelter.

It is this idea that you should choose the order in which you fish the pools according to the state of the water, wind, and sun, that is so important. Too often I see people who routinely start at the top, or bottom, of the beat, and work down, or up, through the pools without a thought. A little planning could transform their chances of success.

So frequently it is the leaving of a pool undisturbed until the conditions are right which can make all the difference. This is particularly relevant to the dread combination of low water and hot sunny weather. If, say, a section of water is shaded by a high bank or by trees in mid-afternoon, leave it alone till then. Other sections you may wish to leave untouched apart from the early morning or evening sessions. If you move a fish from its lie in warm shallow water, by disturbing it while fishing, it is apt to keep on moving, up and out of the beat.

To illustrate the importance of choosing when to fish a pool, a glance at my diary shows that I was fishing at Ballogie, on the Aberdeenshire Dee, on 1 May 1990. This was during a period of very hot weather, with daytime shade temperatures into the 80sF, and cloudless skies all day. At half past eight in the morning, the water temperature was 56°F, rising to 62°F by mid-afternoon. The water level was fairly low at 1ft on the gauge. The section of the beat that I was fishing consisted of the Top, Middle, and Lower Slips, the Rail End, and the Upper, Middle, and Lower Flats. The Lower Slip and the Rail End were both too shallow to be worth trying. The Top Slip, at this height of the water, is a very gentle glide with a glassy surface, and although it held a stock of resident fish, I judged it would be best left to whichever of my friends was due to fish it in the evening. The Middle Slip has faster, and more rippled water, and is shaded by the trees on the high bank above it in mid-afternoon. All three Flats are fast stony

Clothing

Fishing is well nigh impossible without proper protective clothing to cope with weather conditions such as this heavy rain at Ho on the Vosso in June, or this blizzard on the Dee in February.

Reading and exploiting the water

Top: Heavy water and a dusting of snow on the top half of the Lummels at Birse on the Dee. The fish are more likely to be in the gentler current lower down the pool.

Bottom: Bright sun and low water on the Lower Inchbare at Ballogie on the Dee. The fish will run up through and lie in the deeper water on the nearside of the pool.

Reading and exploiting the water — time of day

Top: Always try to fish as the light fades in the evening. The magic hour of dusk at Anne's Seat on the Aberdeenshire Don.

Bottom: "During the next 1½ hours I caught three fish there" (page 39, Reading and Exploiting the Water). Note the contrast between the shaded right bank and the glare of harsh sunlight on the left bank.

Views of the Vosso in Norway

Top: Rurholm and School House pools.

Bottom: Looking downriver at Ho Hul while a thunderstorm crosses the lower part of the valley. A vast backwater on the left hand side of the pool is said to be 127 feet deep.

water, with a broken and rippled surface.

In times of low water, if you cannot find shade, fast water with a broken surface is the next best thing. So I chose to fish the Flats till mid-afternoon, when I intended to move up to exploit the shaded Middle Slip. I lost a fish after a few seconds play in the Top Flat, and another after about a minute in the Lower Flat, where I also had a pull from a fish, which took some line from the reel, but no more. When fish are running fast, which they will in low warm water, such pulls, plucks, lightly hooked, and lost fish are commonplace. Do not let a stream of abortive contacts, or lost fish worry you; it is not your fault.

At a little after half past three, I moved up to fish the Middle Slip, which, by now, was nicely shaded. During the next one and a half hours, I caught three fish there in rapid succession, which just shows the importance of choosing when to fish each particular pool. If I had been standing there, disturbing the pool by fishing it in brilliant sunlight when those fish arrived, it is unlikely that I would have been so successful, as they might well have chosen to carry on swimming, rather than stopping for a rest.

The ability to recognize good, or potentially good holding water, is of great importance, and comes with experience. The more that you study the beat, the easier it will be to identify those stretches of water that might be attractive to salmon. So every day when you walk between the pools, or sit by the riverside munching your sandwiches, look closely at the river, and think. How deep is the water? How fast is the current? Are there rocks, or other irregularities that might provide shelter to a resting salmon? What would it look like with a foot less water flowing through it? Or with an extra foot, or even several extra feet of water? Once you have got into the habit of looking at a stretch of water in this way, it will make a big difference to your salmon fishing success.

Where salmon will rest, and the path that they will follow, as they move upstream through the runs and pools of a stretch of river, will depend on the water conditions at the time.

In low to medium heights, salmon will swim up the main body of water, where it is deepest and fastest, in the runs and stickles between the pools. They will also tend to lie in, or close to, the main current in the pools, depending on how strong that current is, and how warm the water.

In cold water, the fish tend to prefer deeper and slower water. As it warms up, they will also be found in faster, and shallower water. This is not to say that in cold water you will not come across salmon in fast and turbulent streams at the tops of pools. You will, occasionally, but your best bet will be the more even paced water.

Good taking water for the salmon fly is typically between about 4 and 8 ft deep. In very warm water you will sometimes take fish in what seems to be ridiculously shallow water. On a handful of occasions, I have hooked salmon in less than 2 ft of water while fishing on big rivers. This is less than knee deep, and

I have actually stood in the exact spot where the fly was taken to measure it, after dealing with the fish. This happened twice in one week in 1990, in very hot weather in early May, and on both occasions in brilliant sunshine during the middle of the day.

This does not mean that salmon will forsake the deeper and slower stretches when the water is warm. Far from it. In very low water, all the fish may have been forced for security to take refuge in any really deep water that is available. This may be in narrow pools in gorges, or in holes carved out of the rock below a fall, or where the river has scooped out a deep channel under a rocky face. These refuges may be very deep, sometimes more than 25 ft. Many hundreds of salmon may shelter in these deep holes. They are not usually the simplest of places to fish with the fly, and sadly, they are easy targets for the sickening activities of gangs of poachers with tins of cyanide.

There are several reasons why these pools are often so difficult to fish well with the fly. Firstly, because they are so narrow, it is often difficult to get the sunk fly down near the level of the fish. Secondly, although it can see the fly on the surface perfectly well, the salmon may, quite literally, not be bothered to swim up through 20 feet of water to attack it. Thirdly, if it did so, it would lose its place in the densely packed ranks of fish. Fourthly you may not be able to put your fly over the fish at all. In some gorges below falls, there are caverns extending for many yards beneath the rock on which you stand on each side of the river, and in these caves, sheltered from above by up to several yards of rock, there may be hundreds of fish, secure from any legitimate attempt with the fly. Other deep holes may be almost still, and it can be difficult to present a fly attractively in these places without disturbing the fish. So, in low, warm water, you may have to concentrate on those stretches where you can present your fly attractively, but where there are fewer fish, in the hope of finding one that is either running, or resting briefly. This may be more productive than flogging away at larger numbers of fish resident in very deep water.

The pace of water as it flows down through the pool will vary. At the top of the pool, the fast and turbulent head stream is unlikely to hold fish for long, unless the water is either very warm or very low. In cold water the fish will probably wish to lie alongside rather than in it. Towards the middle and tail of the pool, the stream is likely to be slower, and the fish, even in the coldest of water, may be happy to lie in it. The tails of the pools, where the water starts to speed up again, can be highly attractive to fish when water temperatures are above about 40°F, but below that temperature, the fish may prefer the slower water in the body of the pool.

This is not to say that in cold water you should ignore the faster head and tail streams of the pools. Always start fishing a good distance above where you think the best water starts. Even doing that, I am not infrequently surprised by salmon taking my fly in the first few casts, often when I have extended less than half a dozen yards of fly line beyond my rod tip. (This is another argument in favour of a stealthy approach to the water.)

When the river rises, the paths followed by the fish as they swim between, and through the pools will change. Greater water volumes may mean that the fish prefer to swim up along the side of the main current, rather than forcing their way up through it. This will obviously change the places where they lie in the pools, as well. Places where the current was previously too slow to be attractive, or where the depth of water covering the lies was insufficient, now become attractive to fish. So you will then have to concentrate on different sections of the pool, and areas which you formerly dismissed as being too shallow, or too slow, may now become your best chances. As the water rises, productive areas will increasingly tend to be places which have a more gentle stream flowing through them due to their being sheltered from the main force of the current, by, for instance, groups of large rocks, or a bend in the river. In low water you should keep an eye out for such strategic signs.

In very high water, when the river is chugging along level with the top of the banks, the fish will be forced into any quieter areas alongside the main flood. They will frequently be found creeping upstream within a yard of the bank. In sections where the banks overhang the stream, they may be under the overhang itself. Look for areas of gentler water, often extending only a few yards from the bank. The width of this taking water may be less than the length of your rod. Areas which, in low water, were no more than stretches of bare, uneven, shingle with the occasional large boulder, and which you walked across dry-shod to fish the main river, can be transformed by an extra six or seven feet of water, into the most productive stretch on the beat. When you see such areas of shingle, look especially for signs that they may be sheltered from the full force of the current, by, for example, a point sticking out into the current further upstream, or a group of large boulders (which in themselves could form a high water lie), or by being below the inside of a bend which forces the main current on to the far side of the stream.

Look carefully at large boulders that are partially or completely exposed at low water. If there is a depression carved in the shingle by the force of the current either alongside or behind the rock, this could well be a high water lie for a salmon.

To illustrate the way that the position of the areas in which you are most likely to find a taking fish will change at different heights and temperatures of the water, I have drawn a number of sketches.

Fig. 2 Main taking areas in low warm water.

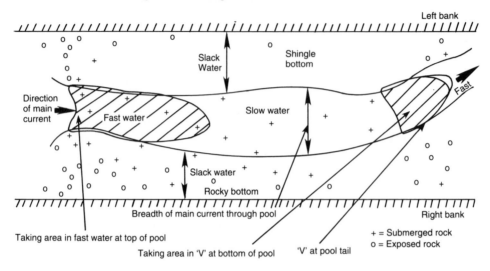

Figure 2 shows a pool in low warm water. The main taking areas are confined to the fast water at the top of the pool, and the 'V' at the bottom of the pool where the stream starts to narrow, and gathers pace again. Where the current broadens and slows in the main part of the pool is less likely to be productive water, although, if it is deep enough, fish may be resident throughout the season.

Fig. 3 Most probable taking areas in low cold water.

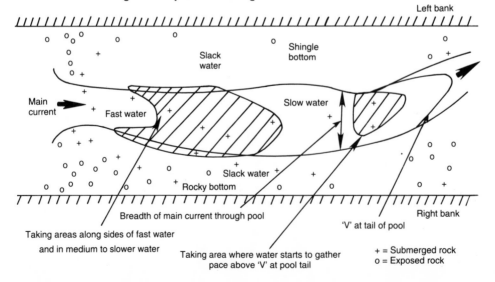

In cold water, the fish are less likely to be found in the fastest stream, and will probably be distributed in the medium to slower paced water, as shown in Figure 3. This shows the fish tending to lie along the edge of the main current near the top of the pool, and also in the area where it broadens and slows in the main part of the pool. Lower down, in the very slow water, it may be too shallow, and the stream too slow, to be productive even in cold water. The fish will also tend to lie slightly above the 'V' at the bottom of the pool, rather than actually in it as they do when the water is warmer.

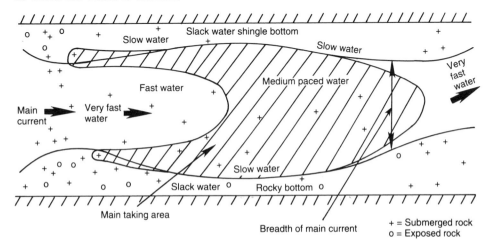

Fig. 4 Main taking areas. Water above average height, low 40°sF.

Figure 4 shows the dramatic increase in the amount of productive water in this same pool when it rises to medium, or above average water heights. This is what is meant by the "best height" for a pool, that is to say the water level at which the productive fishing area is at a maximum; or that level at which certain highly favoured lies are likely to be occupied by salmon and can be fished in the most attractive manner. Figure 4 also shows the fish lying on the edge of the fast water, behind the rocks at the top of the pool on both sides of the river. These narrow strips of water often provide temporary holds for fish that pause briefly on their way up the river, and should always be fished with care. The diagram shows the distribution of the best taking water at a temperature somewhere in the low 40sF. If the temperature was another 10°F or so warmer, the productive area would extend further up into the fast water at the top of the pool, and it would also tend to be rather narrower in the main body of the pool, with the fish not lying in quite such quiet water close to the sides of the river. However, if the water is more than a little coloured or dirty, or one is fishing late in the evening, fish will often be taken in the very nearly slack water at the sides of the pool. In cold water (less than 40°F), the fish may not lie quite so far up the pool, nor right down into the 'V' where the water picks up speed at the tail of the pool.

The 'best height' for any pool will depend on its shape. The width of the pool, and its slope (the difference in height between one end of the pool and the other, divided by the distance between the two ends), will largely determine how well it fishes at different water flows. Ignoring special features in any particular piece of water, a narrow, steep, sloping pool will tend to fish well in lower water, whereas a broader pool with less of an incline will tend to fish better in a medium or higher volume of water. Some pools may not be deep enough to hold fish well in low water, and other pools may not have enough obstructions to break the force of the current in high water. Hence my repeated call for careful observation to determine the characteristics of any one stretch of water. A pool may have two or three distinct, and widely separated heights at which different areas fish well. In between these distinct water levels, it may be poor and unproductive.

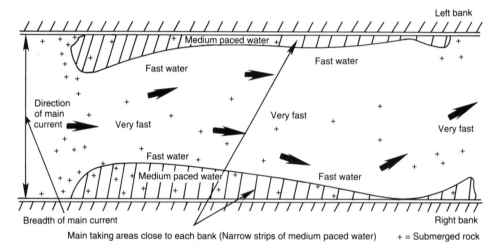

Fig. 5 Most probable taking areas when river running bank high.

Figure 5 shows the same pool after a substantial rise in water level, so that the river is now running bank high. The water rushing down through the centre of the pool is now much too fast to form an attractive lie for salmon, and the main current fills the entire width of the river. However, the groups of the now submerged rocks, on either side of the river at the top of the pool, break some of the force of the water, slowing it down so that there is an area of medium-paced water behind them. Alongside both banks, the turbulence, caused by irregularities in their surfaces disrupting the flow, slows the water so that the strip of medium-paced water also extends along each bank. The strip of productive water on the right bank is wider than the strip on the left bank, because the rocky bottom, strewn with large boulders, helps to slow the water over a wider area. In these high water conditions, the fish run more slowly, and will frequently pause in such strips of water. To improve his reading and exploitation of the water, the angler should try to understand the fish's point of view, and think that if he were a salmon, what routes would he follow at different river heights and temperatures? What would be attractive long term holding water, and where might he choose to stop for a brief rest as he travelled upstream? In high water, which path will avoid the fastest and most turbulent flows? In low water, he will navigate by following the heaviest current, and avoiding the slacks. If he enters the pool at a particular point, how will he move through it, so that he will be correctly positioned to find the line of least resistance to the next pool up? Where is the largest area of deep water that will offer security in time of drought? At intermediate heights, where is the water that is neither too fast nor too slow? How might changing temperatures alter his view of what constitutes attractive water?

In trying to adopt the fish's viewpoint, the angler will rapidly gain a greater understanding of his quarry, which will improve his ability to successfully read and exploit the water.

Concealment

The salmon is a wild animal. It is not like the stocked fish, e.g. brown, or rainbow trout, that are released into lakes, reservoirs and southern streams. Before their release into the 'wild', these stocked fish are accustomed to the sight of humans moving about the sides of their tanks and ponds, and afterwards, they are always less wary than their totally undomesticated cousins. Despite this, many anglers appear to take much more care to conceal themselves from stocked trout than they do from wild salmon.

Salmon have excellent vision, and can also feel vibrations through the water, such as a heavy footfall on the bank, or the grate of a wading stick, or studded soles on rock. When alarmed, their initial reaction is to sink a little lower in the water, both to increase their concealment against the bed of the river, and to improve their field of vision. This response may escape notice by the casual observer, who might believe that the fish has not seen him; but a fish thus frightened is unlikely to take a fly.

When the fish is seriously alarmed by the approach of an intruder, it will lie on the bottom of the river with its tail bent round, ready to provide the lightning acceleration to take it to safety. Only if the intruder gets too close will the fish make its dash for deep water or other sanctuary. This initial reluctance to move from its lie is in sharp contrast to the behaviour of the trout which, when alarmed, tends to make an instant departure, either swiftly, or with a gradual drift, depending on the nature of the approach. This misleads people into believing that salmon are less wary than trout. The salmon is a large fish, and it will draw more attention to itself, if it moves in a small, or shallow water, than if it stays still and relies on concealment. So, just because you can see salmon lying motionless on the bottom of the river, do not think that they are undisturbed by your presence on the bank.

Concealment is as important in salmon fishing as it is in the pursuit of brown trout in the clearest of chalk streams, so take great care when walking along the bank of a pool before fishing it, and especially so if there is any chance of fish lying close in. Try to keep at least ten yards back from the water.

Because of refraction and reflection, distant objects at a shallow angle above the surface of the water will be difficult for the fish to see clearly, whereas objects at a steeper angle (i.e. higher up), above the water surface, will be much more easily seen by the fish. Since the water surface is almost always rippled, I think that it would be pointless to quote precise angles of vision, but, if any angler wishes to find out more about the subject of what fish can, and cannot see, through the surface of the water, let him read *The Trout and the Fly* by Brian Clarke and John Goddard.

If you stand on the top of a steep bank, you will therefore be more visible to the fish than if you are standing at the bottom of the bank. If your rod is moving in a vertical plane during casting, it may be more visible to the fish than you are yourself. So, beware of rod flash. It may look smart to have a high gloss finish on your rod, but a final coat of matt varnish will reduce the risk of disturbing the fish.

A high bank above and behind you provides background to help conceal yourself from the fish. If silhouetted against the sky, you will be much more visible. When you are fishing with a long line (over 30 yards), and especially if you are deep wading, you will be far enough away from the fish you are covering, not to have to worry too much about concealment from them. However, you should take care to disturb the fish that are lying close to you in the water as little as possible. You may want to fish the pool a second time, or someone else might be waiting their turn to come down behind you. Do not disturb the fish from their lies by wading down through the middle of them, and especially not in low warm water, when they might forsake the pool, and the beat as well.

When lying in at least six feet of water, salmon seem less disturbed by a pair of wader-clad legs moving slowly past in the water, perhaps seven or eight yards away. In shallow water (less than four feet deep) this would be more than close enough to drive them from their lies. So pay special attention to stealth and concealment on small rivers, and on larger ones in times of low water, because there is no doubt that under these conditions, salmon are easily frightened by the angler's presence.

Some fishers advocate 'resting' a pool, by giving it half an hour, or an hour's respite between each occasion that the pool is fished down. In general, I don't agree, but this is obviously subject to some provisos. The smaller the river, the shorter the pool, the lower the water, and the closer the fish are to the bank you are fishing from, the more likely it is that your passage down the pool may have alarmed or disturbed the fish, with the result that it may be sensible to allow them time to settle down and relax before you try again. Sometimes it is almost impossible to fish the pool properly without passing too close to the fish, and in such places it is wise to try elsewhere for a while, before returning to make another attempt. But most of the time, and particularly on larger rivers, 'resting' a pool simply is not necessary. Many pools will be large enough, so that even if you do disturb the fish in the top of the pool, sufficient time will have elapsed before you finish at the tail for those at the top to have settled again, so that you can return and restart straightaway.

While fishing the pool down, it is a good idea to try and restrict the amount of false casting you do. A line flashing over the surface of a pool, or worse still, a fly and line smacking into the water during false casting, can certainly startle salmon. So, acquire the habit of getting your casting right first time. To this end, learning to do the Spey, and double Spey casts will help you immensely. If you are not already a competent Spey caster, then do, please, visit a properly qualified casting instructor.

It is sensible to use a dark-coloured line such as green or brown, for sunk line fishing, because it will tend to be seen against the background of the bed of the river and the water near it. For the floating line, I favour a light colour because, when it is over the fish, it will be seen against the bright background of the sky. A light-coloured line also helps the angler to see it against the surface of the water, which is vitally important for the control of the movement of the fly. To this end, I frequently use pink-, or orange-coloured floating lines, which are especially visible in the evening. The fish should normally see the fly before it sees the line, which will be separated from the fly by up to 15 or more feet of leader. This should mean the end of the line is far enough away from the fly for the two not to be linked in the mind of the fish, and for the line, no matter how brightly coloured, not to disturb the fish while the fly is over it. The impact of the line landing on the river seems to worry the fish more than the passage of a brightly coloured line through the water over their heads.

Loch fishing for salmon is a different matter. Here you will be retrieving the line towards yourself, so that the fish will often see the line before it sees the fly. The fish will also tend to be lying in shallower water than is often the case in river fishing, so it will have a smaller 'window'. The fish's 'window' is the area of the water surface through which it can see the world above. Outside the area of the window, the fish will see the reflected image in the under-surface of the water, of the bed of the river or loch, otherwise known as the 'mirror'. Again, for a fuller explanation, I refer the reader to Brian Clarke and John Goddard's book *The Trout and the Fly*. Because the fish has a smaller window, it is more likely to see the line against the background of the 'mirror'. This reflection will tend to be dark-coloured, so a light line will contrast strongly, and be highly visible to the fish. This accounts for many people's preference for a green or brown line for loch fishing, and they are quite right. In calm shallow water, a dark line will be less visible, and disturb the fish less than a light line.

Under normal circumstances, the repeated passage of flies, either sunk, or near the surface, does not seem to worry salmon unduly. The exception is where the fish have been subjected to repeated attempts to foul hook them. Some sections of rivers in the Borders, and central and southern districts of Scotland are notorious for this despicable practice, which, in the worst cases, is carried out blatantly, and in broad daylight by large numbers of poachers on town or Association water. In some areas, such contemptible, and indeed criminal, behaviour appears to be deliberately ignored by bailiffs or other regulatory authorities. In these circumstances, where fish are repeatedly being raked by weighted trebles, sometimes without even a pretence of dressing as a fly, salmon become extremely nervous. The appearance of even a small fly on a floating line may result in all the fish in the pool milling about in confusion and alarm. This anxiety is rapidly transmitted through the fish, so that even newcomers that have not been previously subjected to the barrage, become frightened. Unless trapped by desperately low water, the fish will not stay in the pools when subjected to this abuse, and will tend to move on at the earliest opportunity.

Sometimes salmon do appear to get used to the presence of anglers, or other people, on the banks. In the chapter entitled Persistence, I relate how I had been standing in full view of, and casting over, the same small group of fish for well over two hours in the same place, before catching one of them. I am convinced that those fish had simply grown accustomed to my presence, making the same movements in the same place, and to the regular splashes of lure and line, and that after this length of time, no longer considered them a threat. However, I am not convinced that this is a particularly common occurrence, and would generally recommend a stealthy approach to the water at all times.

In times of low water on small rivers the salmon will feel particularly vulnerable, as they are often virtually trapped in a pocket of deep water, with no real means of escape through the surrounding shallows. In these conditions, you should use every means possible to hide from the fish. Keep low, and never allow yourself to be silhouetted against the skyline. Use all the available cover, such as boulders in the river, or on the bank, or bushes, trees, and long grass to hide from the fish. Casting from a kneeling, or sitting position will help a lot. Be prepared to crawl into position if necessary. Use the bank of the river as background by keeping below it wherever possible. Although the river may be less than 10 yards wide, and need little more than a rod's length of line plus your leader extended to cover it adequately, you may well do better by casting down to the fish from 20 yards or more upstream. Accurate and controlled casting is vital. The flicker of the line during a false cast, or the splash of a bungled attempt may wreck your chances for hours. It is better to sit and think what you are going to do for several minutes, rather than charging in regardless.

One great advantage of doing your reconnaissance the day before you start fishing, is that you will not be alarming the fish by blundering along the bank on the day itself. You will already know where it is particularly important to keep back from the water's edge, and will have planned your route to maximize your concealment when approaching any especially difficult pool. You may also have found out where, by crawling on hands and knees, and cautiously extending your rod over the water, you can dibble your fly over a fish lying within a yard of the bank, and not approachable by any other means with any chance of success. Watching a salmon suddenly rise rapidly through the water, with its mouth open, to attack your fly, engulf it, and turn down again, all within a few feet of yourself peering through the grass on the bank, is one of the greatest thrills that salmon fishing has to offer. It cannot be achieved without great attention to concealment and stealth.

Do not forget your motor car when approaching your fishing. Many salmon rivers have rough tracks close to the bank along which one can drive to fish some of the pools. There is no doubt that the fish will see a large, moving object like a car, particularly if it is on the top of a steep bank overlooking the pool. Sunlight will be reflected from the windows and shiny paintwork of the car, and may flash on the surface of the pool. If approaching the river by car in the evening, switch off your sidelights before they are visible from the surface of the pool. Try to park some distance back from the edge of the bank, so that interior courtesy lights, for instance, will not be visible from the water, when the car door, or boot, is opened. When turning your car, make sure that you reverse away from the river. If you reverse towards the river, the white reversing light, and red stop lights may well be visible to the fish. It is important to remember that to the fish, you, your car, and its associated lights, are unfamiliar objects, and the sudden appearance of any unfamiliar object will be treated with alarm. Fish often lie closer in to the bank during the evening, and it is foolish to risk disturbing what may be your only chance of the day.

Concealment from the fish is important not only to help you hook the fish, but also to help you land it. While playing your fish, try to stay out of its sight, as this will often shorten the fight. So frequently, a fish that seems to be giving up, and to be ready for the net, or for beaching, catches sight of its would-be captor, and makes a panic-stricken dash for deep water. This often adds several minutes to the playing time, greatly increasing the chances of a last minute loss. Keep down while you are playing the fish. Wear dark, or dull clothing to blend into the bank behind you. If I am netting a fish in a suitable place, I will often try to hide behind (downstream of) a large boulder, so that both I and my net are concealed from the fish. Then when I bring him down past the rock, the first that he will know of my net is when he is actually inside it.

Some anglers appear to believe that concealment is unimportant. I have heard of a few, and read of others, who think that salmon need to be woken up before they are worth fishing for. These anglers resort to tactics such as repeatedly swimming a large dog through the pool, or throwing in a brick attached to a cord, and hauling it out again at ten yard intervals down the bank, or beating the surface of the water with branches. Their argument seems to be that once a fish is settling down after being frightened, it will be more alert, and therefore more likely to respond to the angler's lure. Nothing in my experience leads me to accept this argument. If the fish is still in a state of heightened awareness, it is still frightened, and therefore an unlikely taker. Secondly, if you disturb the fish from their lies, they are apt to keep on swimming — up and out of the pool, and probably out of the beat as well. Fish in a fish farm go off their feed if frightened or stressed, so why should anybody expect a different response from a wild fish? The only thing that I want to wake up the fish, is the sight of my fly moving over their heads in a lifelike way, with all its hair fibres flickering in the current.

Wading and wading safety
Wading skills form an essential part of the successful salmon angler's approach. Wading can enable you to cover more of the productive water of a pool than you could from the bank, and to position yourself where controlling the fly will be easiest. It can also help concealment by keeping you off the skyline.

It also teaches you about the geography of the river bed, and the set of the currents. Knowing that there is a depression scooped out of the shingle beside or behind a rock, so that it can only be waded past in safety on one side, may tell you that it is also a potential high-water salmon lie. As you discover the best wading routes down a pool at different heights, you are also building up a map of local knowledge which you will be able to exploit as conditions change. A deep boulder-filled slack may be unpleasant wading in low water, but transformed into a series of most productive lies when the river is higher. Where the current changes direction, so that it swings across the pool, may be a natural stopping place for salmon in low water, but the quiet area beside it may be better in high water. Wading with your eyes open, and your mind alert, so that you think about the changing depth and nature of the river bed, and the varying pressure of the current, will help you understand the pool, so that you can exploit it better.

Every year I watch people wading down pools that could be more easily fished from the bank, and marching straight through the middle of the fish they are trying to catch, thus disturbing them from their lies. A few moments observation and thought about whether it is necessary to wade, and whether it will improve the way you cover the fish, before setting foot in the water, is much better than habitually charging straight into the pool as deep as you can go. It may be more productive to cover the fish on your own side of the stream with a short line, than wading in up to your neck to cover the ones that splash so temptingly on the far side.

Wading safety is an important consideration, and much has been said on this subject by a variety of authors, such as Hugh Falkus in his book *Salmon Fishing, A Practical Guide*. To minimize repetition, my comments must be brief.

All salmon anglers should be able to swim competently both on and under the water, regardless of whether they wade, or fish only from bank or boat.

Familiarity with underwater swimming will prevent disorientation if you are tumbled head over heels in a heavy stream. If you cannot swim, some form of buoyancy aid ought to be given more than serious consideration. However, they do have some disadvantages. Those that are slim enough to be worn comfortably through a day's fishing are generally not buoyant enough. Those that are buoyant enough are often too bulky for practical use. Those that are equipped with an automatic inflation device are always at risk of inflating accidentally. They must be worn on top of all the angler's clothing, because if they are inflated under any other item of clothing, there is a risk of the angler being strangled. Automatic inflation devices that are triggered by contact with water can be set off by standing in pouring rain for several hours. Toggles, for inflating the life jacket can get caught up in nets, clothing, or other items of the angler's equipment. Accidental inflation of the life jacket while trying to land a salmon would be more than a little distracting!

Neoprene waders are made from closed cell foam rubber and are more buoyant than some of the leading brands of buoyancy waistcoat. Divers usually need several kilos of lead to overcome the buoyancy of their neoprene wetsuits, and I happily rely on my waders to support me. Wearing a belt round your waders, or a raintop fastened outside them will also be an aid to buoyancy, by keeping air trapped inside and slowing the inrush of water.

The security provided by a wading stick is important to many anglers. The staff should mainly be used as a probe to investigate the bottom of the river ahead of the angler's feet. It should be used to identify obstacles such as boulders, and find ways round them. It can measure the depth of water, and save the unwary from a step into a sudden hole. It is also a valuable prop, supporting the angler so that he is less likely to slip, trip over a rock, or lose his foothold in the current. However, it is unwise to become too dependent on one, or to acquire the habit of leaning too heavily on it, lest it slip suddenly. It is safer to keep your weight on the foot that is firmly anchored, while moving the other, rather than bearing down heavily on your staff. Beware of using one to enter water so fast that you cannot stand without the stick's support. Getting out of trouble in that situation is much harder than not getting into it in the first place.

If you do fall in and are swept out of your depth, here are a number of points to remember:

1 If your head is under water, hold your breath until your head is back up above the surface. This is common sense, but many people who fall in, promptly inhale! You will bob up to the surface in a few seconds.

2 Do not close your eyes because you are under water. Open them so that you can see where the surface is and give a couple of kicks to help reach it. (Shutting one's eyes is an instinctive response by many people. Deliberately opening them will mean that you are not giving in to panic.)

Do not worry about losing your contact lenses if you wear them. Keep a spare pair with your emergency change of clothing.

3   Lie on your back in the water with your toes just breaking the surface. Although the back of your head will probably be in the river, your mouth and nose will be clear. If properly clad, you will ship surprisingly little water, and float fairly high on the surface. Floating down the river like this is actually very comfortable! Always try to stay horizontal, not vertical in the water.

4   Hold on to your rod. Losing it will add insult to injury. Some hollow glass or carbon rods are positively buoyant, and will float even with the reel attached. In any case, if you cannot swim, you can use the butt of your rod a bit like a pole on a punt, to push yourself towards the shore.

5   If you are being swept down a rapid or over a waterfall, make sure you go feet first. This will significantly reduce the risk of bashing your head on a rock.

6   Never try to swim against the stream because you will make little headway and simply exhaust yourself. Swim squarely across the current. It is surprisingly easy to make good progress by just kicking your legs while lying on your back. You can also use your arm to help paddle yourself towards the shore.

7   Try to conserve the buoyancy of waders and clothing.

8. Do not lower your legs in the water to feel for the bottom. This allows air to escape from your waders, reducing precious buoyancy.

9   When your body is bumping the bottom of the river, or you have kicked your way to the bank, turn over and crawl out of the river and up the bank on hands and knees. Then remove your waders while sitting or lying on the bank. If they are full of water, they may be too heavy for you to stand up in.

10. Once safely ashore, make use of your emergency bag of clothing as soon as possible, to get out of your wet things. There is nothing to be gained from squelching around any longer than you have to. A plunge into the sun-warmed waters of the summer months will probably not impair your ability to carry on fishing, once you have dried off. In early spring it is a different matter. Falling into icy water can be a severe shock to the system, with hypothermia as the consequence. If you do suffer this misfortune, get to the nearest place where you can have a hot bath and some hot food, as soon as you can. If possible, get someone else to drive you, as hypothermia will impair your coordination, concentration and rationality. If, after you have warmed up, you find that you are still tired, then I suggest you retire for the day, rather than returning to the river bank to fish.

However, after all this advice on what to do if you fall in, I would suggest that it is better not to fall in at all! It is easier to fall over in shallow water than in deep water, because there is less support for your body. Also people tend to move more hurriedly and less carefully in shallow water. If you are careless, it is much easier to trip over a rock, although, unless the current is very fierce, you are less likely to come to any harm.

It is a good habit to plant a stick at the water's edge before starting to wade. Keep an eye on it as you move down the pool. Even the biggest of rivers can sometimes rise at a really frightening rate. On several occasions I have seen the Dee rise by a couple of feet in an hour, that is nearly an inch every two minutes. On one occasion it rose at nearly twice that speed. Had I been standing out in the middle of the river without realizing what was happening for even a few minutes, I might not have been able to get back to the bank without a swim. One has to be especially wary on rivers that are used for hydro-electric generation, where the sudden release of 'generating water' can mean a very dangerous, and extremely rapid rise.

A rising river does not just mean that the water is deeper. It means a stronger current, which is what usually makes the wading more difficult. A pool that can be waded comfortably at 2ft on the gauge may be impossibly fast when the water level is above 2ft 6in. If the river can rise that amount in only a few minutes, take care.

Be careful too when fishing a whaleback in any kind of rising water. This is a submerged ridge of rock, or bar of shingle running downstream, with deep water on both sides and below. Having waded out through shallow water to the top of the ridge, to fish the stream on the far side, one then wades down the ridge. Having reached its downstream end, one has to turn round and wade back up it, before being able to return to the bank. Just because you can wade out to, and down, a whaleback fairly easily, it does not mean you will be able to get back up it to safety. Even a gentle rise in water levels may catch one in an alarming situation.

Always stand with your legs aligned up and down the current, rather than at right angles across it. Your upstream leg will shield your downstream leg from the force of the current. If you stand square across the stream, your water resistance will be much greater.

Standing in the lee of a large boulder, even many yards downstream of it, will help protect you from the force of the current. Be careful when picking your way round them in strong currents. The stream may have scooped out a hole around the sides, or immediately downstream of the boulder. So do not take an unwary step into water a couple of feet deeper than you expect.

Take small steps and move slowly, keeping your weight on the foot that is firmly planted till you are sure that the other is securely in place. In really fast water, you will have to shuffle, sliding each foot along the bottom. Usually, I move the upstream foot first, and then "catch up" with the downstream foot.

The natural response of many people in a strong current is to try to brace themselves by bending their legs at the knees. This can make things worse for two reasons. Firstly, bending the knees increases the surface area of the angler below the water, which gives the current more to work on, and thus increases the pressure. Secondly, bending the legs increases the amount of body weight below the surface, with a corresponding decrease in the amount above it. Since the density of the human body is approximately the same as that of water, the weight of the submerged mass of the angler will effectively be negligible. It is only the weight of that portion of his body that is above the surface that is holding him in place. It is often better to stand on tiptoe, relying on the strength of calves and ankles to resist the current, than it is to bend the legs at the knees. Standing on tiptoe raises a little more of the body weight above the surface, thus improving the security of the angler's foothold. It also lessens the area beneath the surface on which the current can press. However, when negotiating a boulder-strewn bed in deep slow water, it is easier, and safer, to bend your knees, to help reduce the chance of a slip.

Do not stand on top of boulders in the river, however conveniently situated, as they can be deceptively slippery. Generally it is much easier to climb up on to a rock than it is to get back down into the river. The rock may be unstable, loosely resting on the bed of the river, and it may tilt unexpectedly, to plunge you into the water.

Do not stand too near the edge of a bank of shingle that slopes steeply down into the deeps. It may be tempting to gain that extra yard or two, and stand on the slope below the edge, but it is inevitable that the shingle will slide from beneath your feet. As you try to climb back up, every frantic step will simply dislodge more shingle.

Try to move softly and with deliberation, to avoid disturbance. Minimize the amount of splash. Try not to scrape your wading stick over rocks, and beware of studded soles crunching on the bottom. Fish will hear these alarming sounds a long way off, outside casting range in calm water. Standing in the fast stream at the top of a pool in low water may alter the strength of the current further down, and thus disturb the fish. Be alert to the fish's viewpoint.

Be very careful when you have to stand on ice rather than on the bank or bed of the river during a period of exceptionally cold weather. Ordinarily one cuts off the ice down the side of the pool with a spade before starting to fish. If the ice is thin enough it can be broken with heavy sticks. However, if the ice is not broken every day, it will soon become too thick to break, and the angler will be able to do no more than widen the main channel of the pool, and fish while standing on the ice. Doing this over deep water on a river is dangerous. Because of the currents, the thickness of the ice may vary from more than two feet to less than two inches in the space of a few feet. From above, there may be little to suggest any sudden thinning of the ice beneath, especially if it is all covered by a layer of snow. If you fall through the ice into deep water, you will not be able to break your way up through the ice from underneath.

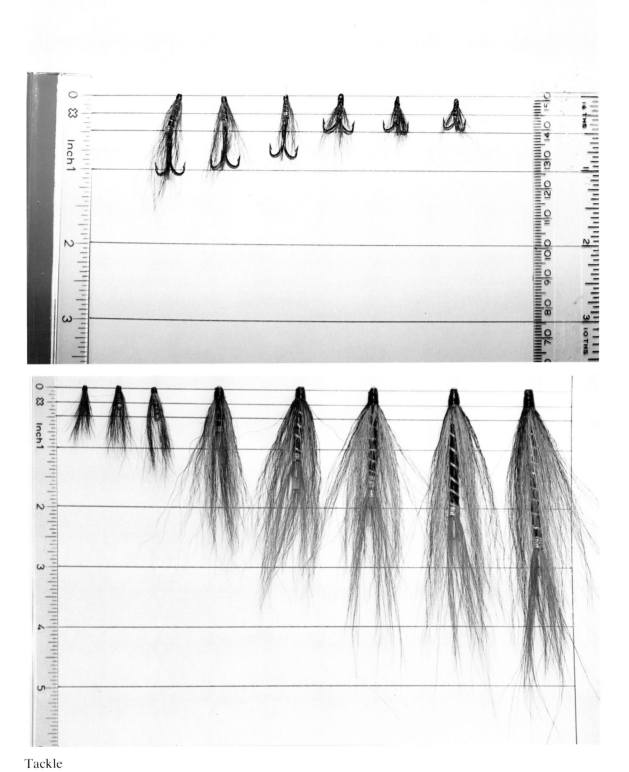

Tackle

Top: Hairy Mary tubes and trebles from ½″ tube down to the smallest of trebles.

Bottom: Drowned Mouse and Hairy Mary tube flies. Note how far the hairs of wing and tail extend beyond the end of the tube, so that a 1″ brass tube means a fly with an overall length of 2½″–3″.

Tackle

Top: The author making an underhand back cast prior to the overhead forward cast with an ultrafast sinking (700 grain) shooting head at Skorve Osen, R. Vosso. Fishing a large fly close to the bottom in 30 or 40 feet of water is relatively easy with such tackle.

Bottom: Even on small rivers, a long rod may be very useful in manoeuvring flies (and fish) around the rocks. The author fishing the Dart in Devon.

Wading

Top left: Careful not to wade too deep, the author fishes the sunk line in the Cruives Pool on the Naver. Minutes before the picture was taken, he caught a salmon from this same stance.

Top right: Handlining an ultrafast sinking shooting head on the Vosso. Note that the author's legs are aligned up and down and not across the stream to reduce water resistance.

Bottom: Wading slightly further in and casting well downstream can reduce the risk of small flies fishing too fast in swiftly gliding water by helping to avoid a downstream belly in the floating line. The author single speycasting at Chelamy on the Naver.

Water conditions

Top: The Dee roaring down in spate (7½–8 feet on the gauge). Fish can still be caught at this height in sheltered water close to the bank. In the flood mentioned on page 6 (The Fish), the river's height was around 15–16 feet on the gauge.

Bottom: "Quiet flows the Don . . ." August on the Bridge Pool at Monymusk, when accurate casting and a delicate approach is vital to success.

An American was fishing at Kincardine O'Neill one year, during just such a period of hard weather. He fell through the ice and was swept away beneath it by the current. He survived by demonstrating a remarkable degree of calmness under pressure. Unable to break his way up through the ice from beneath, he swam out under it till he reached the clear water flowing down the middle of the pool and was able to surface. If only anglers were all as level-headed as that.

Fatal accidents are very few in relation to the hours of deep wading involved. I suspect that crossing a street is far more risky than braving the waters of the Spey. When I fall in, I usually bounce out again before I become seriously wet enough to require the services of my emergency set of clothing. I have even taken an accidental dip while fishing on crutches, with a broken leg encased in plaster from my toes to the top of my thigh. If you fall in, you will float, and I have had the necessary practice to prove it!

Part 3 — Presentation

Section 1: General Theory — Dynamics and 'J' Curve Presentation

If you fish the same piece of water with a group of friends over several years, a casual study of catches and the methods used will reveal an interesting fact. A single pool, under identical conditions of water height, temperature, light, etc., will produce fish to various anglers using different fly sizes but otherwise similar tackle. For example, Angler A may fish the pool with say a size 4 fly and catch salmon; Angler B fishes the pool with a size 6 fly and catches salmon: as does Angler C with a size 8 fly. Is this another perplexing example of the salmon's inconsistent behaviour? The answer is, no: quite the reverse in fact. It is an example of consistent behaviour, of a predictable response to varying stimuli.

How can this be true? In all cases, the water height, temperature, clarity and speed relative to the fish, were identical. Similarly, the direction and intensity of ambient light, and atmospheric conditions in terms of air pressure and temperature were the same for all three anglers. The only thing that could differ was how each angler fished his fly. The way that the fly is fished governs its speed relative to the water, and to the fish, and this allows an explanation of why each angler was successful, and why the behaviour of the salmon was consistent in their taking three different sizes of fly under the same conditions.

If the fish is lying in water flowing at 5 miles per hour, a fly held stationary in the current will effectively be moving at 5 m.p.h. relative to the water, but at zero m.p.h. relative to the fish. However, a fly dropping downstream at the same speed as the water, will be moving at 5 m.p.h. relative to the fish, but at zero m.p.h. relative to the water. If a fly is cast square across the stream, the current will cause a downstream belly to form in the line. Because the angler is holding one end stationary, this will cause the other end, i.e. the fly, to be dragged downstream at up to twice the speed of the current, just as if the middle of the line was running over a pulley that was being dragged away from the angler. This means that the fly could be moving at up to 5 m.p.h. relative to the water and up to 10 m.p.h. relative to the fish. If, however, the angler continually flicks an upstream curve into the line, to prevent the current forming a downstream belly, the fly will move down more slowly than the water. If the angler slows his fly in this way (the process is known as 'mending' the line), his fly may be moving downstream at, say, 3 m.p.h., and this will be its speed relative to the fish, but the fly will be travelling at 2 m.p.h. relative to the water.

This is all relevant to the expected behaviour of small animals in the water. A little fish, or shrimp, say an inch and a half long, could not maintain its station in a 5 m.p.h. current, and would tend to be swept downstream. It could possibly manage that speed for short bursts lasting only a few seconds, but its sustainable speed would probably be no more than 1 or 2 m.p.h. It would therefore tend to drop downstream at about 3 m.p.h. with occasional brief pauses when it accelerated to hold its position against the current. However, a slightly larger fish, say 5 or 6 inches long, could more easily maintain station in such a current. It would not be forced downstream to anything like the same extent as it moved across the pool. The salmon will therefore expect a small fish, perhaps 5 inches long, to move straight across the pool without being washed downstream, and even to manage the odd upstream dart against the current. It will also expect that a smaller fish, perhaps an inch and a half long, would travel downstream at a slower rate than the current, perhaps occasionally managing to briefly hold its place in the stream. This suggests that an angler should fish different sizes of fly at different speeds to trigger a taking response from the salmon. It also accounts for the success of the different sizes of fly used by Anglers A, B and C in the same place and under identical conditions. With their distinct styles of fishing, Angler A chose a larger size of fly, and fished it fairly fast across the pool. Angler B chose an intermediate size of fly, which he fished at a medium pace; and lastly Angler C chose a smaller size of fly which he fished at a slower speed relative to the water.

It is this idea, that for any set of environmental conditions there is a range of fly sizes that will be successful, if fished at the correct speed relative to the water, and to the fish, which is so important. I refer to it as the dynamics of salmon fly presentation. It is a concept that unites the use of a fly with an overall length of 3in being stripped in fast across a pool, and the use of a fly with an overall length of just 1in being drifted down and across the same piece of water.

Once the angler has grasped this idea, it opens up a vast range of different tactics available to him, for varying his approach to fishing any particular pool. It also tends to make rather a mockery of simplistic tables linking fly size to water temperature. For instance one such table, included in the work of a well-known author, which I have open before me as I write, suggests that with a water temperature of 39°F one should use a fly with an overall length of 3in, and with a water temperature of 55°F, one should use a fly with an overall length of 1in. This may be sound advice if your imagination, and your ability to control your fly, are limited. By way of contrast, I can, for example, recall a bitterly cold April morning on the Dee, with, as we said at the time, snow showers on the hour, every hour. The water temperature was 39°F, and the air temperature several degrees lower in a biting north-east wind. I caught two salmon (12 and 14 lb) and lost a third, all on a $^3/_8$in tube with an overall length of 1in. With the water temperature in the middle 50s, one of my standard techniques, for use on days with a downstream wind so strong that I cannot effectively mend the line upstream, is to use a 1¹/₂in tube fly, with an overall length of nearly 3in. I cast this square across the pool, and fish it very fast, stripping in line by hand if necessary, which may result in the fly feathering in across the surface of the water towards me. This can produce some spectacular takes, with the fish throwing themselves out of the water, and engulfing the fly as they plunge down on top of it. One has to be prepared to release the line in a hurry on some occasions to avoid a break. I remember one 18¹/₂-pounder that hit the fly at what felt like 60 m.p.h., wrenching the line from my fingers. The reel first screamed and then shrieked as the line peeled off it. Fearing an overrun, I foolishly tried to slow the reel by pressing my palm against the rim. For an awful second, before I got my hand out of the way again, I thought that the rod or the leader, or both, must break. Fortunately, neither did, and I landed the fish.

If these were isolated examples of fish taking a small fly in cold water, or a large fly in warm water, contrary to the accepted pattern, one could dismiss them as flukes. But they are not, because I find that such events are regular occurrences, fitting the anticipated response of the salmon to the predicted movements of different-sized organisms at varying temperatures.

Water temperature and the speed of the fly in relation to the water and to the fish, are important factors to take into consideration when deciding what size of fly to use for the style of presentation selected. Because the salmon is 'cold-blooded', its body temperature is approximately that of the surrounding water. Therefore, as the water temperature rises, so will the metabolic rate of the fish, which become increasingly active as the water progressively warms up, and more likely to attack faster moving or more distant prey. At low temperatures, the fish are more sluggish, and therefore less likely to pursue small, rapidly moving prey, especially near the surface of the water in a fast flowing stream. However, they can be persuaded to attack a small, slow moving target, and this is especially likely in a more gentle current.

Many people forget that it is not just the salmon that is slowed down by low water temperatures, but its potential prey will also be slowed down. This means that a small fish, perhaps 3in long, that could easily hold its place against a 4 m.p.h. current with a water temperature at over 50°F, would probably tend to drop slowly downstream in the same current if the temperature was 10°F lower.

In cold water, a larger fly may be needed than in warmer water, in order to look natural to the salmon, when the lures are moving at identical speeds relative to the water, at each temperature. However, a small fly can still catch salmon in cold water if the water speed is not great, and the fly is moving slowly in relation to the fish.

Because both the salmon and its potential prey are slowed down in cold water, and become more active in warmer water, the angler should either progressively reduce the size of his fly as the water temperature rises, while keeping his lure at a constant speed relative to the water; or, he can use the same size lure, and gradually increase its speed relative to the water, at successively higher water temperatures. Conversely, as the water temperature falls, the angler can either use a progressively larger fly at a constant presentation speed, or he can use the same size fly at slower speeds relative to the water and to the fish, in a similar manner to a natural organism whose speed of movement is reduced by declining temperatures.

However, there are limiting factors in the dynamics equation, and these are the practical speeds of fly presentation. Firstly, in very cold water, it may not be possible to show the fly in the desired manner. If, for instance, it is possible to present a small fly at a slow speed relative to the fish in a medium-paced current, the fly may still be moving too fast relative to the water flow for it to look natural to the fish. In this case the angler must increase the size of his fly till it is the size of something that would be able to hold its place in the current at that temperature. Another limiting factor is the reluctance of salmon to move up from the bed of the river to take a fly near the surface in very cold water. I do catch fish on the small fly on the floating line in water temperatures around 40°F, but only where the modest pace of the water permits this approach. However, when temperatures are significantly lower than 40°F, results tend to be better if the fly is brought down close to the level of the fish. This often means that in addition to a sinking line, a heavier, and therefore larger fly will usually have to be used. If a larger fly is used, it can obviously be fished faster than the smaller fly that would have been fished near the surface.

In warmer water, there are practical limits to the speed at which flies can be drawn through the water, and still form an attractive presentation. At water temperatures in, say, the mid 60sF, a fly that is only a couple of inches long becomes, effectively, a very big fly, and has to be fished as something that could hold its place in even the fastest of currents, while in slower water it has to be stripped in at high speed. There is obviously a limit to the speed of a potential prey organism relative to the fish, above which the salmon may not bother to attack. There is also the disturbance factor. Casting large lures, and hauling them back across the pool is more likely to disturb the fish than a more delicate approach with a smaller fly. Water temperatures in the mid 60sF usually imply very low water levels, which tend to magnify the problem of disturbance.

However, in these high water temperatures, the use of a moderately large fly, fished fairly fast, can have significant advantages over a very small fly fished more slowly. The advantages are the larger hook size, and the fact that this allows the use of a stronger leader. With water temperatures in the mid 60sF, the normal fly size will be around 12–14. While this may be fine for a grilse of 5 or 6 lb, a fresh fish of over 15 or 16 lb is more likely to be lost, as the small hooks might not have a deep enough hold to prevent their gradually tearing free during a prolonged struggle. A larger hook may get a deeper hold that is less likely to result in disappointment, particularly if the fish are fresh, which means that their mouths are softer than if they have been in the river for some time.

Sometimes in cold water, but more frequently as the water warms up, it is possible to persuade salmon to take a lure moving at high speed relative to themselves, and moderately fast relative to the water. This is the fly travelling rapidly down, and across, the stream. As a method, it is directly comparable to the use of the upstream minnow when spinning. If a fly is cast square across the river, and a belly allowed to form in the line, so that the fly is dragged downstream faster than the pace of the current itself, this will represent a small potential prey animal actively swimming downstream. The salmon only has a very brief period in which to make up its mind whether to attack or not. Here again, because the fly is moving fast relative to the fish, a larger than normal fly size will be used, depending on the speed and temperature of the water. In cold water (less than 40°F) this can mean the use of lures more than 6, and sometimes up to 9in in overall length, depending on the presentation speed. In warm water the length of fly used for these tactics will become progressively smaller, shrinking to something of 2in or less by the mid 60sF.

Other factors that can influence the size of fly are the amount of ambient light and the clarity of the water. As the light fades in the evening, it pays to use a slightly larger fly than during the day. If I have been using a $^1/_2$in tube during the day (overall length about 1$^1/_4$in), with the floating line, I will first of all use something fractionally larger or more heavily dressed, and then, as the dusk deepens, I will tie on a $^3/_4$in tube, with an overall length about 1$^3/_4$in, assuming that I present my fly in the same way. This is not to say that during the evening you cannot catch fish on the same size fly that you used during the day. Quite frequently I experiment by leaving, say, the tail fly unchanged, and alter only the size of the dropper, to find that I still catch fish on the tail fly when it is practically dark. However, I am happier using a larger size fly, because at low light levels it is difficult to see accurately what is happening to the line and fly, and precise control becomes more difficult. This means that in the evening, despite my best efforts, I may still be fishing the fly faster than I did during the day, and this might account for the success of the larger fly.

Clarity of the water may occasionally have some impact on the size of fly chosen. It would perhaps help to explain what I mean by clarity in this context. Dissolved substances such as peat stain, no matter how black the water, have almost no effect on the size of the fly one should use for any given presentation. However, suspended matter in the form of mud from field washings etc., can be more important. Ignoring the fact that muddy water usually means a rise in level, and therefore a faster flow, its effect will depend on exactly how muddy it is. However, if you can see a white stone on the bottom, in a couple of feet of water in ordinary daylight, the fish will probably be able to see your fly near the surface in several times that depth. In these conditions, I tend to use a more heavily dressed fly than normal, usually the same size, but occasionally a size or two larger than I would ordinarily select for that height of the water. If the water becomes less muddy, I will rapidly revert to the usual size of fly for whatever style of presentation I have chosen.

So far in this chapter, I have stressed the need for precise control over the way that the fly is moved through the water. Whether you are hand-lining a large fly back across the pool, or drifting a tiny fly down the stream, you must be aware of what your fly is doing, and that the pace of the current varies in different parts of the pool. You will therefore have to constantly adjust either the speed with which you strip in the line, or the angle of your rod to the water, and the amount of the upstream, or downstream belly in your line. Fishing in this way requires far greater concentration and mental effort than the traditional down and across, chuck it and chance it method, that is practised by so many. The realization that altering the presentation of your fly is as important as changing its size, in response to varying conditions, will significantly affect the way that you approach your salmon fly fishing.

To achieve this control over your fly, you have to be able to manipulate your line on the water with ease. For most of your fishing you may want your fly to drop down the stream more slowly than the current. This gives you the opportunity to 'hang' your fly in the stream, to make it pause tantalisingly in the current above the salmon, before it starts to drop slowly down the stream again, just as a little fish or any other small creature would behave.

To make your fly drop down the stream more slowly than the current, you will need to have an upstream curve, or 'mend', in your line. Because you are stationary, holding one end of the line, you will act as a tether, effectively slowing the downstream progress of your fly as the current straightens the curve from the line.

You may need to make the initial mend immediately after casting. This is how to do it. Finish the cast with your rod pointing fairly high above the surface of the water, usually at an angle of about 30–45° above the horizontal, depending on how fast the water is. The high angle will keep your line out of any fast water immediately in front of you, and will also give you some slack line with which to make the mend. (If your line is dead straight, with no slack, and you then put a curve into it, you will reduce the straight line distance between yourself and your fly, that is to say that you will have jerked your fly towards yourself). Then in a continuous motion move the rod tip a little downstream, to help free more line from the surface of the water without disturbing the fly, and flick it smartly upstream, with your rod tip coming to rest slightly lower in the air than it was before, but still pointing in the same direction across the river. Your rod tip should have made a roughly oval movement in the air. Your line should now be lying in a convex curve on the water, with the far end sloping downstream towards the fly. You can now, if you wish, raise your rod back to its original angle above the water, because you may need to repeat the mend every few seconds, to retain control over the fly, and slow its downstream progress.

After some practice at mending your line, you should be able to mend the entire length of it, or which ever part happens to be dragged by the current, at will, in many conditions. Only a strong wind downstream or onshore will present real problems. You will be able to lift your entire line right the way down to the leader, without significantly disturbing the fly. At best, your line should be more or less straight for most of its length, with the bulk of the curve several yards above the end of the line, where it joins the leader. Viewed from above the bank opposite you, the profile of your line on the water should approximately resemble the letter 'J'. There should be a short length of line and your leader hanging straight down the current, followed by the curve in the line, with the main body of the line running more or less straight back across the pool towards you. This is what I describe as the 'J' curve. It is important because it allows you to drop your fly downstream over the fish. This means that the salmon will see your fly first, before it sees the leader, or the line, or their shadows, any of which might put it off.

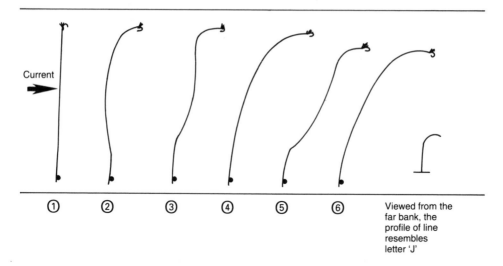

Fig. 6 Mending line to form 'J' curve.

Figure 6 illustrates the 'J' curve.

1 The angler casts almost square across the current.
2 He immediately mends his line upstream to form 'J' curve.
3 The current starts to drag his line downstream.
4 Before the current can drag his fly, he again mends upstream, re-establishing the 'J' curve.
5 Current again starts to drag at mid part of line.
6 Before the current can move his fly, he again mends upstream, re-establishing the 'J' curve.

The process is repeated at will, as the angler allows his fly to move down and across the current to his side of the river. His fly is not inert in the water, but travels down more slowly than the current, just as a natural organism of its size would do. The angler stays in total control of his fly at all times, and can speed, or slow its progress, across, or down, the river as he wishes.

It will also be noted that the angler casts his fly almost square across the river. This is in complete contrast to the 'down and across' school of presentation, which probably evolved because many fishermen either could not, or, more likely, were not shown how to control their lines and flies properly. Casting downstream at an angle of 30–45° from your own bank is going to waste a significant portion of the potentially fishable water on many rivers. Casting nearly square across the river, when combined with the enhanced control of your fly offered by the 'J' curve will maximize your effective water coverage.

As the fly is fished round to your bank, the current will put less drag on your line because of the shallower angle, and you will consequently need to mend less frequently to keep your fly moving at the desired speed. Hence the adoption of the narrow-angled cast by the down and across brigade because it is only in this small arc that their fly will fish properly.

When an understanding of the interaction between the size of the fly, and its speed relative to the stream and the fish and to the temperature of the water, is combined with the ability to control its movement, fascinating new opportunities will widen the horizons of your salmon fishing. You need never be disenchanted with only having a small piece of water to fish. Instead of going down it time and again with the same fly, fished in the same manner, you will be able to vary your tactics through all the permutations of fly size and presentation that your imagination and your tackle can produce.

It will take some time of experimentation and practice to become confident in varying the presentation of your fly. When you begin to experiment with changing the size of your fly, and the way you fish it, do not leave it till the end of a bad day, when conditions have been poor, and you have not seen a salmon in all the time you have been fishing. It is hardly fair to write off a new technique as being too difficult, or beyond your understanding, or a failure for whatever reason, if there are no fish in the water when you first try it. Instead, begin your experiments on a day when you know there are fish in the pool, and you have a good idea of what is likely to be a successful technique in the prevailing conditions. Then, when you try a new method, you can observe the reactions of the fish to your tactics. If, for instance, you fish a larger than normal fly, and there is no response, try fishing it faster, or slower, and see what happens. Gradually, you will build up a store of experience of what method works when, and then you will find that the pleasure you derive from salmon flyfishing expands, as its intellectual possibilities multiply. The more effort you put into solving a problem, the greater the satisfaction when you finally arrive at the solution.

Section 2: The Floating Line

The use of the small fly and the floating line is not the most difficult method of fishing for salmon, but to do it well can demand skills of the highest order. Concentration, dexterity, and precise judgement are needed for the correct manipulation of the line, so that the fly will fish in the required manner. Working out the right tactics to present your fly attractively in a difficult place is immensely satisfying, especially when you at last succeed after many attempts. Part of the joy of the floating line is its visibility on the surface of the water; you can see it at all times, and you know approximately where your fly is at any point. If a fish takes your fly, in all probability you will see the rise as well. This adds to the excitement of a method which offers ease of casting, and greater delicacy, to make it more popular than fishing with the sunk fly.

Floating line fishing in this country was developed and popularised by the great Arthur Wood. Others had greased their lines before him, but he raised the technique into an art of the highest order. Sadly, many modern commentators have misunderstood the descriptions and diagrams of how he controlled his fly. His denigrators write that his fly was allowed to drift downstream, inert in the water. Common sense and more careful reading say that this was not the case, and that he carefully controlled the passage of his fly down and across the river, to mimic the way that any small natural organism would move, fighting the current as it dropped downstream. If his fly had been inert it would rapidly have sunk to the bottom of the river, just like any other small heavy object.

The basis of the philosophy of floating line fishing is again to be found in the salmon's 'cold-blooded' nature. As the water warms up, the fish's metabolic rate increases, and so it becomes more active, and thus more likely to swim up and attack a small prey near the surface of the water. There seems to be a general consensus that the critical temperature lies in 45–50°F range. Above this critical temperature the floating line is thought to be more successful, and below it, the sunk line. However, I am not sure that the consensus view is entirely accurate, and I feel that the range of temperatures over which salmon will either move up to take a fly near the surface, or will attack a sunk lure, is much more of a grey area than most people believe. To support my views, I offer the following:

1 Thousands of salmon are caught by people spinning (i.e. using a large sunk lure) each year, when water temperatures are above 50°F.
2 A large sunk fly is often the preferred method of people fishing, when the water is just starting to fall, and clear, after a summer spate. In these conditions, water temperatures are obviously well above 50°F.
3 I catch salmon on a small deeply sunk fly, using nymph-style presentation, when water temperatures may be well over 60°F.
4 In the previous section of this chapter, I related how I regularly catch

salmon on the floating line, at temperatures well below 45°F. In the range 40–45°F I expect to catch around one-third of my fish on the floating line, on the days when I use both methods, despite probably using the sunk line for at least three-quarters of the day. (The disproportionate amount of time spent fishing the sunk line is due to my perverse character. The sunk line is more difficult to fish well than the floating line, and I therefore get more pleasure out of using it, and so fish it for longer.)

5 Even with water temperatures down into the upper 30sF, a surprising number of fish are caught on the floating line during the last half-hour of dusk. Even if I have caught a fish on the sunk fly earlier in the evening, I still like to try the floating line for that final half-hour. It has worked too often to be a coincidence.

Over the years, I have come to believe that correct presentation is the crucial factor, and that getting the dynamics right is often more important than whether you are fishing floating or sunk line techniques. A well presented fly near the surface, of the right size in relation to its speed of movement relative to the water and to the fish, and the temperature of the water, may succeed when a less well presented fly fished with the sunk-line fails. Conversely, the well presented sunk fly will do much better than the poorly presented fly fished on the floating line. Since salmon do become more lethargic in cold water, there is no doubt that the good sunk-line man will beat the good floating-line man when water temperatures are low, but that does not mean that the floating line should be abandoned entirely in cold water. Some pools are desperately difficult to fish with the sunk line, but relatively easy with the floating line, and here you may well do better if you give it a try. Always be prepared to have a go with the floating line during that last half-hour of the day, when the dusk fades into darkness. Incidentally, you do not need to use a vast fly when fishing the floating line in cold water, as night falls. My standard size, even in these conditions, is a $^3/_4$in tube, with an overall length of about $1^3/_4$in. A faster presentation will of course demand a larger fly.

I do disagree with Arthur Wood in some areas, notably in the use of a dropper. He did not use one, but I do for almost all my fishing with the floating line. Only in low water is there a significant danger that if a fish is hooked on the dropper, the tail fly, trailing in the water, will become fouled on a rock or other obstruction. It is rarer for the dropper itself to get caught up. There are some days when the tail fly catches all the fish, and others when only the dropper is successful, and others still when the results are evenly divided. I have not yet heard of, nor arrived at any consistent explanation for this, and all I can say is that at least a third of the fish that I catch on the floating line in any season are caught on the dropper. So, apart from fishing in very low, and rocky water, I always use one for floating line work.

Presentation is so important to success with the floating line, that it begs the question, 'How is it done?' What are the techniques that turn the magic trick that makes all the difference between triumph and failure? To enable one man to 'draw out leviathan with an hook', where others 'have toiled all the night, and have taken nothing'.

Perhaps part of the way to the answer is to look at a number of examples of what I think of as the classic style of presenting the fly on the floating line. The first is one of the easiest, and demands little skill to fish properly.

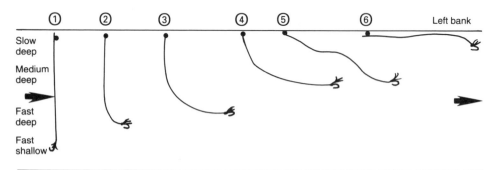

Fig. 7 Slow water close in, fast water further out.

The angler is fishing from the left bank. Immediately in front of him the water is deep and slow-moving. Further out it is still deep, but moving at medium pace. Beyond the centre line, the river is deep and fast-flowing. Towards the far bank, the depth of the water lessens rapidly, so that it becomes a fast-flowing stony shallow. The majority of the fish lie in the deep water on the left-hand side of the pool, from the edge of the fast stream in the middle, to the slower water quite close to the left bank.

(1) The angler casts nearly square across the pool, so that his fly lands in the middle of the deep fast water. Instantly he mends his line upstream. This, combined with the current moving his fly downstream, produces the classic 'J' curve as in (2). The angler holds his rod nearly square across the water, and at about 20° above the horizontal. This allows him to have sufficient slack to put another mend into the line if required, and to control the speed of his fly as it drops down the edge of the fast water at (3), and moves across the medium water (4). Throughout this time the angler has made sure that it is his fly, and not his leader, which has been the first thing to move into the salmon's vision. Depending on the relative speeds of the water, it may take only one, or it may take several mends to provide proper control of the angler's fly between (1) and (4). If lots of mends are required, it would be sensible for him to go back down the pool a second time with a fly a couple of sizes larger. If little mending is required, he might fish the pool again, but with a smaller fly, and mending more

frequently. When his fly moves from the medium water to the slower water, he may need to make his fly move faster, and to do this he lowers his rod to the horizontal, and moves it downstream so that it is now pointing at his fly as it swings across the current. This will allow a small belly to start to form in the middle of his line, as in (5), which will begin to speed the movement of his fly in towards his own bank (6), where he starts to move his rod point around inshore in front of the fly. This will further help the fly's progress in towards his own bank through the slow water, where he completes the process by slowly drawing in three or four arm lengths of line, prior to casting again.

Because the angler was fishing from slow water into fast, little effort was required on his part to enable him to fish his fly properly. Any tendency for his fly to move too fast will naturally be countered by the stream as his fly is drawn into the slower water. Such a pattern of water speeds is typical of a pool fished from the inside of a bend, where the fastest water moves down the outside edge of the curve. Fishing a corner pool like this from the inside is often very easy, so that no matter what he does, even a complete beginner will find his fly hanging properly in the water for a substantial portion of each cast.

Instead of going down the pool again with a different sized fly as suggested earlier, he might try again with the same fly, but fishing it either faster, or slower than before. To fish it faster, he will mend his line less frequently, hold his rod more nearly horizontal and keep it pointing either at his fly, or inshore of his fly. To move his fly even faster he could start stripping in line by hand, and accelerating this process as the fly moves into the slower water from the medium-paced water. To fish his fly more slowly, he keeps his rod pointing at a higher angle above the water, and more nearly at right angles to his own bank. He mends his line more frequently, as soon as any portion starts to be dragged by the current.

Through his control of its speed, the angler can use the same fly, without changing its size, to fish both fast and slow water. This can avoid wasting a lot of time in changing your fly as you move down the pool.

The next example is the obverse of Figure 7. It is the same stretch of water, but fished from the opposite bank. It is a more difficult situation to master.

The angler has waded into the fast shallow water as far as he can without sliding down the slope into the deep water. It is wise to wade with care in such situations, because if you get too far down a shingle slope, you may not be able to get back up it against the current. As the fish lie on the far side of the fast stream in the medium, and slow, deep water, the angler casts a long line, slightly downstream of square across the pool, and immediately puts a big mend into the line to produce the 'J' curve, as in (1) and (2). He holds his rod square across the stream, and with the point high above the water, to reduce to a minimum the amount that the fast current close to him can drag at the line. The width of the fast water will determine how easy it is for it to drag his line. If the fast water is too wide, it may not be possible to control your line and flies in the slower water on the far side, and so different tactics may have to be adopted. In (3) the current starts to create a small downstream belly in the angler's line, which, if left untended, would soon start to drag the fly at speed through the water. The angler immediately mends his line, and thus prevents any untoward movement of his fly. (4)

Fig. 8 Fishing from fast water close in into slow water further out.

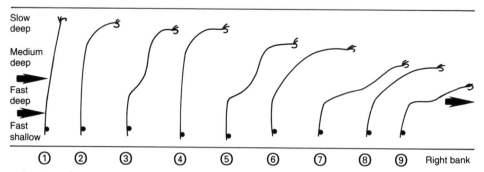

When fishing a fly in this way, it is most important that any mend be made before the belly in the line reaches the fly. If the current grips a section of line, and starts to belly it downstream, mend it immediately. This will avoid disturbing your fly in the water. If you wait, you may not be able to avoid moving your fly when you mend your line.

The aim is to have your fly dropping downstream more slowly than the water, with the occasional small pause while it hangs enticingly in the current, moving at a similar speed, but of course on an opposite diagonal path, to the way the fly was fished from the far bank (or easy side) of the pool in Figure 7. Repeated mending of the line will be needed to achieve this control over the movement of your fly, sometimes as many as a couple of dozen mends during the course of fishing a single cast. Indeed, on some sections of pools with a fast stream on the side I am fishing from, I keep the rod tip moving continuously to create a perpetually rolling loop of line which can keep my fly stationary, or moving slowly downstream as desired, on the far side of the fastest of currents. A breeze blowing upstream and away from the bank on which you are standing is of great assistance in this technique, which is well nigh impossible in a downstream wind.

In Figure 8, the angler continues to mend his line and to control his fly as he allows it to drop slowly through the medium-paced and down the edge of the fast water, as shown by (5), (6), (7), (8), (9). Unless the water is very warm, the salmon are unlikely to be lying in the fast water, and he can allow his fly to swing across it. In some pools of this type, salmon may lie on his side of the fast stream, especially where it starts to slow a little in the body of the pool. To fish this narrow strip, the angler can raise his rod while his fly is swinging across the fast stream, thus drawing the fly upstream, and then when it reaches the appropriate point on his side of the stream, he slowly lowers his rod again to allow the fly to drop back down his chosen line of the current. In some cases it may pay to fish the near side of the stream down with a short line first, before attempting to fish the main part of the pool on the far side of the stream with the longer line.

If the fast stream is too wide, it may not be possible to control the speed of your fly on the far side of it in the manner I have just described. If this is the case, then be prepared to fish a larger, and sometimes a much larger fly, such as perhaps a Collie Dog, or Elverine type streamer fly, which can be dragged across the stream by the current. The larger the organism, the faster it can swim as a general rule, and this is the logic to apply to your fly selection.

Many beats on medium and larger rivers have pools like this that fish well from one side only. It can be rather galling if the anglers on the opposite bank have a pocket of water from where they can catch fish repeatedly, and with apparent ease, while, although you can reach this pocket of water from your own side of the river, you are unable to catch any fish from it. These delightfully challenging situations can keep you amused for many seasons as you struggle to find the solution, and great is the feeling of personal triumph when at last you discover the successful approach.

The next problem to consider is the midstream rock. This is where there is a large boulder in the middle of the current, with salmon lying in several yards of water behind it. Sometimes, depending on the nature of the bottom, and the flow of the water around the rock, the fish may also lie alongside, or even in front of it. The temptation is to allow your fly to swing across it in the normal way, and certainly fish will be caught like this. However, to maximise the chances of success it really has to be treated as a number of different lies, to each of which the fly must be presented in turn (Figure 9).

Fig. 9 The midstream rock: Floating line fly presentation.

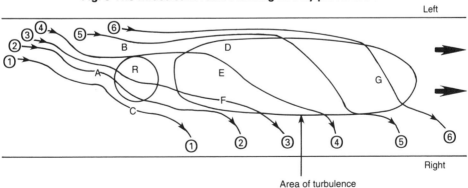

Figure 9 shows a submerged rock, R. Occasionally, salmon will lie in front of it at A, and sometimes alongside it at B and C. However, they will normally lie behind it, beneath the area of turbulence, D, E, F, G. The angler should cover the fish on the nearside of the stream first, and let us assume that he is fishing from the right-hand side. As his fly fishes down and across the pool, the angler keeps an upstream mend in his line, and his rod point fairly high above the surface of the water. He allows his fly to drop down more slowly than the current towards A, where it hangs for a second or two. Then the current starts to straighten the mend from the line. Lowering his rod tip a little, he then flicks another small upstream mend into his line, and moves his rod tip a small way downstream and inshore. This allows his fly to drop down past A and over C, as shown by track (1). Next cast (2), the angler drifts his fly down the stream over A, but then, by keeping his rod stationary, and allowing the mend in his line to partially straighten, his fly is swung diagonally down and across the rock, where he mends again and allows his fly to slip down the nearside edge of the turbulence behind the rock towards F, as shown by track (2).

Careful study of the different paths that his fly follows with successive casts (tracks (3) to (6)), shows that the angler is mostly dropping his fly down between the edge of the turbulent water behind the rock and the current flowing past it. This is exactly the path that any small organism would follow if it was being swept downstream, which is what the salmon expects to see. If you watch a hatch of large flies, such as March Browns or Olives, being swept downstream on the surface of the water, you will see that they behave in this way, moving down between the outsides of the eddy behind a rock and the current flowing past it. This is what your fly should do.

Fish salmon lies like this with great care. A rock, with an area of turbulence behind it extending over several yards, may take a dozen or more casts to fish properly. However, fished with the surface line in this way, it is much more likely to produce a positive result than simply allowing your fly to swing across the eddy. Only if you are using a larger fly, which can be fished more rapidly, should this latter course be followed.

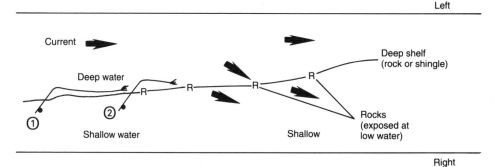

Fig. 10 Rocky shelf running downstream.

Another area that frequently causes difficulty is the rocky shelf running downstream, separating deep and shallow water. This is shown by Figure 10.

Here the fish lie alongside a rock or gravel shelf. In moderate to high water this presents few problems, because the rocks are well covered by water, and the angler at (1) can present his fly by standing upstream and allowing it to dangle alongside the shelf and over the rocks. He can make his fly sway over the fish in a most tantalizing manner by allowing it to drift over into the shallow water, then raising his rod and drawing in a few yards of line, before mending his line out into the current again. This will take his fly out into the stream, and down along the side of the shelf, which can be a very effective way to tempt a fish lying there.

However, in low water this will not be possible, because the current will tend to pull his line in against the rocks which now stick out of the water. If he fishes in the same way as before, his fly will get hung up with every cast, and he must change his approach to avoid this problem. It is time to use the short line. With less than half a dozen yards of line out, plus his leader, as at (2), the angler can use his long rod to lift his line over or around the rocks at will. He has precise control over how his fly fishes, and can drag it over the surface, or make repeated short casts to manoeuvre it in any way he chooses, allowing it to drift downstream, or to dangle in the current alongside the ledge, or be drawn back out into the stream. The short line is both an effective and an entertaining way of presenting the fly.

With the short line, a cautious approach is vital, and maximum concealment is necessary to avoid disturbing the fish, which may be less than a rod length away from you. Bent double, or crawling on hands and knees, you may have to slide into position, and cast while either sitting or kneeling in the water. It can have its lighter moments though. One pool that I fish regularly in this way has the main road running along the far bank, and I know that the sight of me crawling around in the middle of the river sometimes causes consternation among passing motorists. On one occasion, I was bent over and shuffling into position on my knees, when I heard a voice from the far bank asking if I was all right? The occupant of a passing car, a kindly soul, had thought something must be the matter from my position hunched up in the water. I assured him that I was fine. He then asked if I had lost anything, obviously assuming that I had dropped something in the water, and was searching for it on hands and knees. 'Not yet', I replied helpfully, and left it up to him to work out whether I was referring to fish or my sanity. Shaking his head in puzzlement, he retired. Less than a minute after he drove away, there was a small, splashy rise and I was into a fish.

However, fishing such a lie from the opposite bank is much more difficult and will depend on your being able to wade out far enough to cast downstream at quite a shallow angle, to cover the salmon properly. Accuracy in your casting is vital, and a contrary wind may make things very tricky, if not impossible. If I can do so, without getting my fly caught up on the rocks and shingle, I like to overcast slightly, so that the fly lands in the shallow water beyond, and well upstream of the rock at which I am aiming to allow my fly to drift past. I then put a big upstream mend into the line, but with slightly excessive vigour, so that my fly is given a small jerk, which draws it back into exactly the place that I want. The need for precision can not be overemphasized. A few inches away from the correct position can make all the difference between your fly getting caught up in the rocks, or its being in the right place, or its not being far enough over, so that it is ignored by the fish.

With your fly correctly positioned, you can allow it to slide downstream parallel to the rocky ledge, and more slowly than the current flowing past it, as the mend in your line is gradually straightened. You can also release a bit of extra line by hand, to extend further the distance your fly travels down at the right distance out from the ledge.

Some situations may not call for any casting at all, and include fishing some pools in gorges and gullies, and the narrow head stream running into the tops of other pools, especially in low warm water. In these places, from a stance above the top of the fishable water, you can slowly let out your line to take your fly down the pool or run. Moving your rod tip from side to side, and occasionally flicking a mend into the line, you can move your fly across or down, or have it hang stationary against the current, as you require. Again, you might need a stealthy approach to get into position, but one of the joys of this kind of fishing in narrow gullies is that you may have seen the fish in their lies from above before you started fishing. You will therefore know the precise position of the fish, and be aware of when your fly is over them. If you have a companion, or a gillie, who can observe from a hidden position, and supply a running commentary, it can be very amusing. The description of which fish does what, when your fly comes over it, can be most enlightening. Sometimes you can have as much fun being the observer as being the fisher. You will certainly learn a lot about the behaviour of salmon from watching in these circumstances.

I hope that these examples of how to present a fly in different situations illustrate what I think of as the classic style of floating line salmon flyfishing. The essence of the technique lies in the precise control of the movement of the fly. Both the speed of the fly, and the path that it follows down or across the pool are important. The angler must try to match the way that he moves his fly with the expected behaviour of a natural organism under similar conditions of water flow and temperature. Ordinarily this classic style means allowing a small fly to move down over the fish more slowly than the current flowing past. In slower water, the angler can allow his fly to be speeded up, by letting the current create a downstream belly in his line. Occasionally the fly may need a little hand-lining in slow water, to make it naturally attractive to the fish.

The size of fly is determined both by the temperature of the water and by the way that it is fished. Varying the way you present your fly allows you to fish a range of different speeds of water with the same fly, or to use a number of different sized flies on the same piece of water. Similarly by changing the presentation you can fish the same fly at successively higher or lower water temperatures, or use smaller or larger flies at the same temperature. With a water speed of, say, about 4 or 5 m.p.h., my basic fly sizes for the classic style of presentation at different water temperatures are as follows:

Temperature	Tube size	Length overall	Equivalent single Hook Size
Lower 40sF to lower 50sF	$^{1}/_{2}$in	up to 1$^{1}/_{4}$in	4– 6
Lower 50sF to upper 50sF	$^{3}/_{8}$in	up to 1in	8–10
Upper 50sF to mid-60sF	$^{1}/_{4}$in	up to $^{3}/_{4}$in	12–14

The overall length includes the treble hook as well as the tube and dressing.

As I have previously said, it is not just the sizes of the flies that are important, it is the way they are fished that matters. Drifting a $^{1}/_{4}$in tube across a slow flowing pool in the low 40sF has sometimes brought me success, when the use of a more traditional sized fly, or a large sunk fly, has failed for others. I have deliberately kept the above table rather vague because the emphasis should be on how the fly is fished. By manipulating the rod or line, you can infinitely adjust the speed with which your fly moves down or across the pool. The table of fly sizes is no more than the basic guide. When you have mastered the control of your fly, and acquired an understanding of the principles of dynamics, you will have total freedom to decide how much you wish to depart from any standard table of fly sizes. You can then have fun in seeing how far you are able to change your approach, and still succeed in persuading the salmon to take your fly. It is a lot more enjoyable, and intellectually far more satisfying than allowing someone else to do your thinking for you by rigidly adhering to a table of fly sizes and a single method of presentation. You may also find that you catch more salmon.

Section 3: The Sunk Fly

Technically, fishing the sunk line for salmon is much more difficult than fishing the floating line. There are some who dismiss it as spinning with a fly rod. They have a point in that both methods involve presenting a large and deeply sunk lure to the fish. However, the level of skill required to fish the sunk line effectively vastly exceeds anything needed to fish the spinner. Hauling out 30 yards of fast sinking line with a heavy 3in brass tube from the depths along the edge of a backwater, and casting it straight into the teeth of a northeasterly blizzard blowing across the pool into your face, is immensely more demanding than flicking out a heavy minnow with a spinning rod in the same circumstances. The whole process of selecting the right combination of weight (or length) of fly, and the type of sinking line to use, is much more complicated, and demands a great deal more local knowledge, than simply deciding whether or not to add a lead to your line to take your spinner deeper in the water. Control of rod and line is also a far more involved business with the sunk fly than it is with the spinner.

It might be imagined that the sunk fly is most difficult in very high water. In fact it is low water than presents the most problems, and those that catch fish on the sunk fly consistently in low water can count themselves masters of the art. If the fish are only lying in a deep narrow channel because of lack of water, getting the fly down to them, while simultaneously avoiding disturbance or being snagged on the bottom, and still managing to make it fish attractively, can pose a set of problems that would baffle a genius.

In the preceding section, I pointed out that in cold water a proportion of salmon will still rise to take the fly near the surface. However, the proportion of fish that will do so tends to decline as the temperature falls and some of these may also take the fly sunk deep in the water. So, as the temperature falls, fishing the sunk line becomes progressively favoured over the floating line. This does not mean that you have to abandon your floating line in cold water, nor does it mean that you have to discard the sunk line in warm water. The principles of dynamics apply just as much to the sunk line as they do to the floating line. In warmer water, you can still fish the same size sunk fly as you did in cold water, but you will have to fish it faster. Some pools, because of large rocks and other irregularities of depth and current, may be very difficult to fish well with the sunk fly. Until you have mastered the way to fish them with it you may find it rewarding to try them also with the floating line in cold water, if you can achieve a significant improvement in presentation by that method. Do not forget that besides the use of the small fly presented slowly, a large fly fished relatively fast on the floating line often works when water temperatures are below 40°F.

To get the best results from the sunk fly, it has to be fished deep, ideally within about a foot and a half of the bottom of the river. You will have to choose the right type of line, whether it is fast or medium sinking, a sink tip, or even the full floating line, and match it to the correct weight of fly. This is where experience and local knowledge are so important in selecting the appropriate tactics for any particular pool. The aim must be to get the most lifelike presentation of your fly that you can, within such constraints as the depth of the pool, the speed of the water, and the need to manoeuvre your line around irregularities in the bottom.

For instance, in a wide, fairly slow, and moderately deep pool, a $2^{1}/_{2}$in brass tube fished on a sink tip line might get down to the fish as required. However, the speed of the water might be too slow for such a large and heavy fly to fish attractively without hand-lining, which in any case would draw it nearer the surface. In very slow water, such a lure might look about as attractive, and move as naturally, as a lump of lead on a piece of string. A much better presentation might be attained by using a medium sinking line and a $1^{1}/_{2}$in brass tube. The combination of heavier line and smaller, lighter fly would fish at the same depth, but would look far more attractive to the fish. In gentle currents, the mobility of the fly is important.

Fishing a big fly too slowly is one of the most frequent causes of 'near misses'. Plucks, pulls, fish following the fly in from the stream to take on the dangle, and many other half-hearted takes are often the result of the fly being fished too slowly. If this happens to you, try fishing your fly faster, but still at the same depth. This often cures the problem by inducing more positive takes. Otherwise, use a heavier line to fish a smaller fly at the same depth and speed.

The right combination of line and weight of fly to fish at the correct depth must also be matched to the length of the fly and its water speed, taking into account the water temperature. As the water warms up, the salmon will become more active, as will its potential prey. There is a more substantial margin for error using the large flies fished with the sunk line, than with the smaller ones normally associated with the floating line. A 4in fish will be able to swim nearly as fast as a 5in fish, but a 1in fish would be much slower than a 2in fish. The 4in fish is approximately equivalent to the overall length of a Drowned Mouse tied on a 2in brass tube, and the 5in fish equates to one tied on a 3in brass tube. A larger fly will have to be fished somewhat faster than a smaller one to look natural to the fish but the difference in speed will be proportionately less than with small flies and floating line. A fly of the same size can be fished progressively faster as the water temperature rises.

The speed and depth of the water tend to dominate the fly selection process because of the difficulty in controlling a fully sunk line. Once it is fully sunk, it can not easily be mended, and therefore control over the speed of the fly relative to the water is more difficult. It will tend to fish faster than the floating line. Since the weight of the fly is directly proportional to its length (i.e. the longer the fly the heavier it is, for any given gauge of brass tubing) a larger fly will fish deeper than a smaller fly, or it can be fished at the same depth but in faster water.

This has to be balanced with the appropriate choice of line to find the right combination to fish the pool as desired.

At this point, it might be sensible to add a brief comment about the sizes of fly used for fishing the sunk line, which appear to be so large. They are very similar to the sizes of lure used for spinning. The standard 2½in wooden Devon Minnow, when placed on its mount with the usual treble hook and swivel is 3¾in long, almost identical to the overall length of a 2in brass tube. A Blair Spoon or a Toby, when measured with treble hook and swivel, is over 5in long, similar to the 3in brass tube. This comparison can be extended to the way they are fished. The angler using a spinner casts it across the pool, allows it to sink, and then to fish round. If the water is fast, he will not need to reel in. If it is slow, he will. He does this for two reasons: firstly to stop his lure getting caught up on the bottom, and secondly to keep it revolving or wiggling properly in the slow water. In other words, he speeds the passage of his spinner through the water to make it fish attractively. This should also apply to the skilful fisher of the sunk fly.

If you are fishing slow water, you will need to increase the speed that your fly moves through it, or change to a smaller fly. However, using a smaller fly may not always be a practical solution, because it might require the use of a faster sinking line to get the lighter fly down to the correct depth. This heavier line might sink too quickly, and so wrap itself round rocks on the bottom of the river, resulting in the angler continually getting caught up. This is one of the reasons behind my use of a medium sinking line comprised of 20 feet of sinking line spliced to the body of a floating line. Only the front end of the line gets down to the required depth, whereas the body of the line will pass over the top of obstructions. It can also be mended to some extent, allowing the angler more influence over the movement of his fly whereas the standard medium sinker cannot be mended effectively once it has sunk into the water. The standard medium sinker can only be mended immediately after making the cast, before it has had even a second or two to settle into the water. Otherwise one is restricted to hand-lining, and moving the rod tip inshore in front of the fly to speed its progress. When fishing the fully sunk line in slow water, and having cast out across the pool, it is a matter of choosing how much downstream belly is needed to make the fly move fast enough to fish attractively, and putting in (or not putting in) a downstream mend at the start as required. When the fly moves from the midstream towards the slack water at the side of the river, the angler can hand-line in to help it fish properly.

To contrast the need to speed up the movement of the fly relative to the fish and to the water in a slow pool, let us look at fishing the sunk fly in very high water, where the passage of the fly relative to the fish has to be slowed as much as possible. This can be one of the pinnacles of salmon flyfishing, particularly on a river like the Dee, or the Spey, in early May, when a spell of hot weather is melting some of the plentiful reserves of snow on the hills. The air temperature may be in the 70sF, and the water at around 40°F, and running bank high. In shirt sleeves and thigh waders, you fish the big sunk fly from the bank. With the prospect of the occasional pod of salmon moving upstream close to the bank, few thoughts give me greater pleasure.

This high water will be fast moving, and calls for some variation of tactics from those used in slow water. The angler must now try to present his lure at a fairly slow speed relative to the fish, but because the current is so strong, it will be moving fast relative to the water. If the angler holds his rod tip square out from the bank that he is standing on, and he allows his fly to dangle in the stream below his rod tip, where the speed of the current is say 6 m.p.h., his fly will be moving at 6 m.p.h. relative to the water, but 0 m.p.h. relative to the fish. A small fish, or other prey animal, perhaps five or six inches long, could probably hold its place against such a stream for short periods at this temperature, otherwise it might tend to be forced downstream. This is the behaviour that the angler is trying to imitate with his fly.

Fishing with a large (probably 3in) brass tube, and a fast sinking line, the angler casts out, slightly downstream of square, and not particularly far, normally less than twenty-five yards across the river. In his hand he retains a couple of loops of line, perhaps three or four yards. He finishes the cast with his rod pointing high above the water at an angle of about 45°, and immediately puts a big upstream mend into the line, before it has any chance to settle in the water, and takes a pace or two downstream. This allows his fly and line the maximum opportunity to sink into the water.

As the line travels downstream, the mend straightens, but the angler keeps his rod pointing square out from the bank, and above the surface of the water. When the line reaches an angle of about 45° downstream, the angler puts in another upstream mend, shooting the loops of spare line that he has held up till now in his hand.

The angler keeps his rod pointing square out over the river until the line is only sloping out into the stream at a shallow angle. Only now can the fisherman gradually bring his rod tip round inshore, leading his fly slowly over the fish, that will probably be lying less than his rod's length out from the bank. With his rod pointing straight downstream along the bank, he must wait till his fly has completed its journey into the side of the river before beginning to slowly hand-line in the loops of line needed for the next cast. In this very high water, salmon frequently lie underneath the bank itself, and so it is often a good idea to let the fly dangle alongside the bank for several seconds. The first loop of line should be drawn in very slowly, and each subsequent one progressively quicker than the last. Even so, I still occasionally catch salmon that take when I am starting to raise the rod during the cast itself.

When I am lucky enough to be fishing in this manner, I try to keep disturbance of this productive water close to the bank to a minimum. This means casting in a single movement, and avoiding, at all times, any preparatory roll cast parallel to the bank. This implies using the double Spey cast whenever possible in preference to the single Spey, which is nothing like so good in this respect. It also means that when your fly gets caught up underwater in the bank's submerged vegetation, you should use the maximum stealth in your efforts to free it. There may, after all, be a salmon only a few feet downstream from where your fly is snagged, and your next cast will cover the fish if it is not disturbed. It is inevitable that your fly will get caught up in this way when you are fishing from the bank, so take care when you try to release it.

For this kind of high water fishing from the bank, the long rod, 16ft or more, gives the fisher of the big sunk fly a significant advantage over most other methods, including spinning. The long rod allows the angler to control his fly over a much broader section of water than is possible with the typical spinning rod, which is only 10ft long. This ability to hang the fly, so that it is moving slowly relative to the fish, in water that may be quite fast flowing, translates into a most attractively presented lure. It is no surprise that those who fish the big sunk fly regularly achieve such success compared to those who automatically reach for their spinning tackle when the water rises.

As the river level falls, you will usually have to do some wading to get into the best position to fish your fly effectively. Clearly, it is easier to slow the passage of your fly across the pool when it is only moving through a narrow angle downstream of your rod tip. However, just as in fishing the floating line, you may wish to slow your fly relative to the fish on the far side of the pool, but to speed it up in the slacker water on your own side, or the reverse, depending on each pool's configuration.

It is less likely that you will have to release line half-way through the fishing of your lure at every cast, as was necessary in the very high water. However, it is probable that you will still have to make a big mend immediately your line hits the water after casting. Again, just as in fishing the floating line in fast water, you are trying to let your fly drop downstream more slowly than the current itself. A small fish, perhaps 4in long, would probably be pulled downstream in cold water when crossing the main current in a pool, which is how your fly ought to behave as well. When the small fish leaves the fast water of the main current and moves through the progressively slacker water towards the side of the pool, it will first of all be able to hold its own, and then to swim upstream in the more gentle flow. Having slowed your fly in the fast water, let it swing naturally across the medium-paced water, bringing your rod tip round in line with it, and then, in the slower water, moving your rod tip round inshore in front of your line, to help speed up your fly. You might also need to strip in some line by hand. Always, when your cast has fished out to the dangle, strip in several arms' lengths of line, initially slowly, but increasing the pace of each successive length of line that you pull in. This will often tempt a following fish to take the fly.

The greatest variation in the weight of fly and the type of line needed to fish different pools successfully will be at medium water heights. A fast pool of medium depth may need a quick sinking line and a 2in brass tube, whereas other, more gentle pools may require a medium sinker, or just a sink tip, and changes in the size of fly as well. If you manage to fish through the day using just, say, a medium sinking line and a 2in brass tube, you should regard yourself with suspicion. Unless you are truly a master of that piece of water, the chances are that your fly did not fish deeply enough in some pools, and that in others you had to fish it too fast to avoid getting caught up on the bottom. In the former it was too light, and in the latter, too heavy. Frequent changes of line and fly are a chore, but do, please, make the effort. It will make a big difference to your catch.

In order to avoid the temptation of not bothering to change whatever existing combination I may have set up on my rod, I always carry at least two rods whenever I am fishing the sunk fly. If one rod is set up with a fast sinking line, the other will have a medium sinker or a sink tip. This means that I can simply put down one rod, and pick up the other without wasting any time.

Fishing in moderate currents, you ought to move a step or two downstream after finishing each cast. You will probably not want to move downstream during the time your cast is fishing, as this may result in your fly sinking too deep and getting caught up on the bottom. However, while your fly is on the dangle below you in almost slack water, it is nearly inevitable that it will sink to the bottom while you are moving down, especially if you have to take some time to negotiate your path around slippery boulders. What I do to avoid this happening is to strip in the usual five yards or so of line after each cast has fished out, and then re-cast immediately without shooting any of it. I then move down, while keeping the line taut, with my fly coming round fast across the stream, so that there is no chance of it getting caught on the bed of the river. Very soon after I have taken the necessary two paces downstream, I will be able to re-cast, and shoot the spare line in the usual way. Any fish that my fly goes over, during one of these half casts, has already seen it, while it was fishing properly during one of the preceding casts. I therefore do not expect a fish to take while I am moving down, and I have avoided much frustration over the years by using this method. It has reduced the amount of time wasted in freeing caught-up flies, together with the elimination of the associated disturbance to the water, and damage to hook points.

In the autumn, fallen leaves drifting down the river can be a problem, and not just because they get caught up on the fly at nearly every cast on some occasions. The salmon, too, can seem to be bemused by the debris continually floating past downstream, so that they ignore even the well presented fly. The way that I overcome this problem is to use a larger fly than I would need for a standard presentation. This is allowed to sink as usual into the water, then hand-lined back upstream and across the current towards me. This presents the salmon with a lure that is moving upstream, in the opposite direction to the leaves travelling downstream, and which is therefore more likely to attract attention.

As the water level drops from medium to low water, your need for the quick sinking line will progressively reduce, apart from in fast narrow pools, and much of the time you will be able to use a medium sinker or sink tip. Occasionally you will need to use the full floating line with a heavy fly, in order to maximize your ability to lift the body of the line over rocks and obstructions, while keeping your fly at the desired depth. Low water calls for greater accuracy in casting, and planning how to get your fly to do what you want, and where you want it. In many pools, the fish may be concentrated into relatively small areas where there are the correct conditions of depth and flow.

You may have to get your fly to sink in a narrow deep channel, hold it there, so that it fishes slowly across, and then strip in line fast to bring it up in the water, so that it does not get caught in the rocks on your side of the run. Using a medium sinker of the type that I have described, or a sink tip, depending on the depth and speed of the current, wade in as far as you can without disturbing the fish. Then cast downstream at a fairly shallow angle, with your fly landing in the water just beyond the far side of the stream and above where the fish are. Put an upstream mend in the line immediately, and keep your rod out over, and above, the stream. As the mend straightens, allow your rod point to drift round downstream a bit. Your intention is to make the fly sink down in the water at the far side of the channel. The more accurately you are able to do this, the better. Then moving your rod point round inshore, you can lead your fly across the productive water at whatever speed you choose. If the current is slow, you may need to strip in some line by hand.

Choosing the right combination of line and fly, with the precise control of their movement in the water for this kind of fishing, demands technical skills and local knowledge of the highest level. It may take many seasons to learn the proper way to fish the different pools of the beat with the sunk fly in low water. It is for good reason that I believe it to be the most technically difficult method of flyfishing.

Small rivers cause particular problems for fishing with the sunk fly in low water. Avoiding disturbance to the fish, and getting your fly to sink in a restricted space, can test the finest angler. Very often the place where the fish are lying will have a profile that resembles a section of a flooded drainage ditch. That is to say that it may be no more than a channel carved in the rock a few feet deep, of about the same width, and several yards long, and surrounded by water only a foot or so deep. This is a place for the shooting head and single-handed rod. You can use a shooting head with a double-handed rod, but it tends not to be so accurate.

You will need to stand some distance directly above the channel where the fish lie, while remaining as concealed as possible. This may involve kneeling, or crouching behind a boulder. Your shooting head should be a full sinker, but use a light fly, say a $1\frac{1}{2}$in aluminium or plastic tube.

Cast as far downstream as you can — well over thirty, and sometimes over forty yards, is possible for the practised reservoir man, so that your fly, and all the length of the heavy shooting head, land well below the fish. Only the light running line, usually flattened nylon monofilament, should land in the water over the fish. This is to reduce the chance of frightening the salmon by landing a heavy line and fly on top of them.

After allowing several seconds for the line and fly to sink, start stripping in line, to draw your fly up through the channel where you think the fish are, so that it will move upstream slowly past them. The speed with which you do this should vary with the current. You may need to pause, to allow your fly to sink further, once it is in the channel itself. In a moderate stream, you need to move your fly up it very slowly, only a few inches at a time. In a slower current, you will need to make your fly move faster, just as a natural organism would be able to swim upstream against the flow, so that it is presented attractively to the fish. You may need several casts to cover the channel properly, drawing your fly up each side, and the middle, so no water remains unfished.

Using a shooting head often requires a false cast. Try to do this over the side of the river, rather than over the fish themselves. Again, this is to lessen the chance of disturbing the fish.

Another situation where the shooting head can be used, is in fishing wide, slow moving pools on any size of river, up to the largest, in low water. These pools may be very deep, with too sluggish a stream to permit fishing the fly without a lot of hand-lining. A shooting head, fished with either a single-handed or a double-handed rod, because accurate casting is not needed, will outperform the standard double taper. The competent reservoir trout fisher, using a heavy shooting head, and double haul cast, will get his line and fly across the pool with a fraction of the disturbance caused by extending a double taper line with a normal salmon fly rod.

Cast square across the pool. Allow time for your line and fly to sink. This will depend on the weight of the fly and line, and the depth of the pool. Start hand-lining your fly back in across the pool. How fast you do this will depend on how much current there is, the size of your fly, and to some extent, the temperature of the water. The warmer the water, the faster any given size of fly needs to move. It may help you to practise in water close at hand, and to study how your fly looks at different speeds of retrieve. Or it might help to think how fast you would move a minnow of similar size through the water if you were using spinning tackle. In almost still water, with a temperature around 40°F, and using a fly with an overall length of 4in (equivalent to a 2in brass or aluminium tube), you will need to be stripping in about a couple of yards of line every three or four seconds, to make it fish attractively. In other words, your fly will need to be moving at about $1\frac{1}{2}$–2 ft per second. With a fly about half that size, you will need to move it about half as fast.

One other method of helping to speed up the movement of your fly through the water is by backing up. Here you cast across the pool, and then take three or four steps upstream, before starting to hand-line in your fly. Usually you fish a pool down from top to bottom in the usual way, and then back it up from bottom to top. Sometimes, this method can be surprisingly successful. However, unless the bed of the river is very smooth, it is not usually practical to use this method while wading, and it has to be done from the bank, unless a boat is used, as is sometimes the case on the Tweed. Another disadvantage is the danger of the fish seeing you, as you move upstream, before they see your fly. Because of this disturbance factor, the method works best when there is a stiff upstream breeze to put a chop on the water, which will help conceal you from the fish, and the impact of your line on the water surface.

The shooting head also comes into its own when the angler is trying to fish the sunk fly in very deep fast water, such as one finds in Norway. Using my heaviest outfit, which consists of a 16 ft Hexagraph, 23 ft from a reversed 700 grain Deep Water Express shooting head, and a brass tube up to 3in long and 4 mm in diameter, I can cover water of the same depth and strength of current as would be fished by a 1½ oz spoon with another ounce of lead on the trace. By using different densities of shooting head in combination with different weights of fly, the angler can effectively cover almost any water that he would be able to fish with the spinner, including some channels thirty or forty feet deep.

Very high density shooting heads are not difficult to cast with, providing one remembers to swing the fly and line back underhand on the back cast, prior to an overhand forward cast. This makes it much easier to get the timing right than when both back, and forward casts, are made overhand. Using this tackle it is both possible, and tempting to cast huge distances if there is a smooth surface on which the running line can be coiled prior to shooting. However, the angler would be wise to cast only as far as is needed to cover the lies he is trying to fish, and to resist the temptation to try to achieve distances in excess of seventy yards with his fly rod.

Whenever you use overhead casting with the sunk line, regardless of whether you are wielding a single, or double-handed rod, always wear a pair of glasses to protect your eyes. Making a mistake while lifting your line from the water could happen to anyone, even the greatest of experts. If a heavy tube fly strikes you in the face, you could easily lose an eye. So wear a pair of polaroids at all times while overhead casting. It is no bad habit to wear them while Spey casting as well, although this method is vastly safer than overhead casting. It is but a small price to pay for protecting your sight, and in any case they do help you to see into the river.

Success with the sunk line depends not only on getting your fly down to the salmon, but also on making sure it fishes attractively when it gets there. The only times when your fly should be moving slowly relative to the fish, are when the water is fast flowing, or when you are using a relatively small fly. You should treat the old maxim of sunk fly fishing, 'deep and slow', with caution. Deep, yes, but slow, only sometimes. Think always of the speed your fly should be moving through the water to make it attractive. It is easy to fish it too slowly, and you must keep it moving when it comes into the slacker water at the side of the river.

Section 4: The Dragged Surface Fly

The concept of the dragged surface fly groups together a number of techniques that are usually described entirely separately. The range stretches from fishing streamer flies up to nine inches long, down through the arts of dapping and dibbling, to what is known as dry-fly fishing, where the lure may have an overall length of less than half an inch. These superficially distinct styles of fishing have a common theme, involving the movement of a fly in, or on, the surface of the water, thereby creating some disturbance or wake. They are also effectively united by the principles of dynamics, so that the colder the water, or the faster the fly is fished, the larger it should be; typified by the fishing of a big streamer (or longwing) fly, such as the Collie Dog, fast across the surface in early spring. The warmer the water, and the slower the fly, the smaller it should be, as illustrated by the success of drawing a tiny, bushy tube fly, such as a Yellow Dolly, over the surface in the summer months.

The normal method of fishing with streamer flies is to fish them fast across the pool beneath the surface of the water, using floating, sink tip, or fully sunk lines. It is an effective way of varying one's normal floating or sunk line presentation. However, as a departure from this standard approach, for maximum visual impact, and entertainment value, I like to drag a large fly over the surface of the water. It can produce some dramatic takes, with salmon slashing at the fly in apparent fury as it moves over them, even when water temperatures are down to 40°F or less.

If I am toiling away, trying to turn over a full-length sunk line and heavy tube neatly into a contrary wind, it is nice to have a little light relief from time to time. Switching to the floating line and a big streamer fly can be just what is required to sustain enthusiasm and concentration. If the wind then blows my fly and a yard or two of line upstream it does not matter. Effectively it has just put a downstream mend into my line, which is something that I might have had to do anyway.

Dragging a fly over the surface of the water at speed means using larger than normal flies, because they are travelling fast relative to the fish and to the water. At low water temperatures, of around 40°F and possibly below, this can mean using very long flies, perhaps 6–9 inches long, of the Tadpole or Collie Dog type. I happily use extended versions of either my Hairy Mary, or my Drowned Mouse patterns. Whatever you use, cast it square across the pool, and then, either put in a big downstream mend, or allow the line to form a belly in the current. This will cause your fly to be dragged downstream, and across the pool faster than the current itself. In a slow pool, or in warm water, you may have to strip in line by hand as well. The faster your fly is moving at any temperature, the bigger it will need to be.

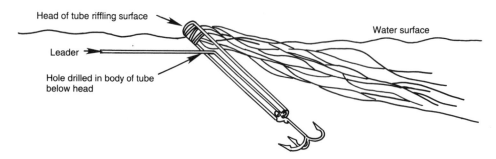

Fig. 11 'Doctored' tube.

To help your fly drag on the surface, you can either use a buoyant, bushy fly, or you can use a light tube. Take a plastic tube fly and make a hole with a needle in the body of the tube a short distance below the head. Thread the nylon leader in through this new hole and attach it to a treble hook at the rear of the tube in the usual way. In the current, its nose will lift, while its tail hangs down in the water. Fished with the floating line it will tend to riffle the surface, making that vital extra stimulus to provoke a taking response from the salmon. These 'doctored' tube flies can be very attractive in their own right, even when fished with the sunk line. This is because they are highly mobile and tend to wiggle about in the water. Their main disadvantage is that they are more prone to tangling the treble hook with the leader than ordinary tube flies.

Salmon tend to take the dragged surface fly thus presented with a wallop. It is either completely engulfed, or totally missed. The plucks, pulls, and nudges that are sometimes so common, when fishing a fly beneath the surface, are much rarer with this method. I have known salmon leap out of the water to attack the lure as they re-entered with a splash, sometimes wholly swallowing the lure. On occasion the treble hook has been so far down in the stomach of the fish that I have been unable to extract it, even with a long pair of forceps. I have had to cut the nylon, and leave the retrieval of my hook till the fish was gutted. However, if you are getting a lot of rises that do not touch your fly with this method, the chances are that either its size, or its speed of presentation, is wrong. Usually it will be because your fly is too big, or you are fishing it too slowly, and you should reduce its size, or fish it faster as a first response. Sometimes, these rises that do not make contact will happen for the reverse reason, i.e. that your fly is too small, or being fished too fast. In either case, a bit of experimentation will usually result in the correct combination of size and speed.

In cold water (below 40°F), the dragged surface fly is not usually my first choice as a method, but it works often enough for me to give it a regular trial. Generally I will fish the sunk fly first, especially when fish are scarce. However, once I have located some fish, ideally several in a relatively small area of water, and if the sunk fly has been unsuccessful (and sometimes even when it has succeeded), I like to try the big fly dragged across the surface. As I have said, it can be a very entertaining and visually dramatic method of flyfishing. Sometimes, it seems to wake up every fish in the pool, causing them all to start jumping at once. Certainly it is fun, which is what flyfishing is meant to be. My ideal temperature for this style of fishing lies above the low 40sF, although I have used it successfully as low as 36°F.

One area in which the technique works well, is fishing the heavy draw at the very tail of the pool, where the water drops over the edge into the rapid leading down to the next piece of holding water. To fish this very lip of the pool, and the few yards of water immediately below it, ideally you should be able to wade out into position, so that no casting is needed, then, keeping your rod point high, you can play the fly back and forth across the current, by moving your rod from side to side. Often, in a lowish water, even on quite a big river, such an outfall from a pool may only be a few yards wide, yet virtually every salmon swimming upstream will pass through it. At the peak of the run, be it spring, summer, or autumn, this can mean hundreds and sometimes thousands of fish in a day. In other words, if your fly is in this narrow piece of water for even a few minutes, the odds are that one or more salmon will have swum past it.

Trailing a big fly across the surface of a heavy stream can often be a way of inducing a running salmon to take your fly in passing as it enters the pool. Most fun of all is when you have a companion who is in a position from where he is able to see the fish as they swim up the run towards your fly. With a commentary, and directions to move your fly to the right or left, or to leave it hanging in the centre of the stream, you will certainly have an entertaining session, with plenty of excitement as each fish approaches, or passes your fly.

Salmon which take the fly on the lip of the pool, or just below it, will often turn and head back down the way they have just come up. Sometimes they will co-operate, and allow you to walk them up into the pool, to play them in the normal way, but often I find that they try to make a dash downstream through the fast water. A good-sized fish, say 15 lb or more, will take some stopping once it is under way in these conditions, and you may have to make a headlong scramble through the boulders, or along a steep bank, to catch up and bring it to a halt, so that you are in control of the situation.

As the water warms in late spring, you will not need to use such a big fly, and if the current isn't too fast, you may be able to use a normal-sized lure for this work, which brings us to the subject of dapping or dibbling. There is no real difference between dragging a large fly across the surface of a pool on a long line, and manipulating a smaller fly on the surface of the water on a short line under your rod tip, other than the distance involved. The same principles apply in matching the size of the fly to its water speed and the temperature.

I always like to think of dibbling and dapping as low water techniques. With a long rod, a short line, and a stealthy approach, it is an excellent method of working the fast water that rushes into the top of the pool. I prefer, as for most floating line work, to use two flies, a tail fly and a dropper. The tail fly acts as a sort of sheet anchor, making it easier to control the movement of the dropper. I make the dropper swim in the surface layer of the water, sometimes drifting it down, sometimes moving it up against the current, or holding it steady as the water slides past, or dragging it bouncing across the stream. By jiggling the rod tip, the fly moves erratically, sometimes making a little jump clear of the water, sometimes briefly sinking under the surface, quite often being half in and half out of the water. The impression you are trying to give the salmon is of a small fish in some kind of difficulty, or a large insect trying to get clear of the water.

Quite often, despite all this attention to the dropper, the salmon will take the tail fly. Sometimes the angler may not even notice the rise to the tail fly, because he is concentrating so hard on the dropper. This happened to me the first time I tried dibbling for salmon. This was in 1982, and I was fishing the Middle Gannet at Ballogie on the Dee. The water was low, and I was using a 15-ft carbon rod, borrowed from a friend. With a stiff upstream breeze, the rod was long enough to keep the flies in position on the far side of the main current, while I stood behind a rock that protected me from the force of the stream on the near side. By keeping the rod point high, and making maximum use of the breeze, I kept sliding the dropper down the edge of the turbulent stream, and then, slowly skating and bouncing the fly up the slacker water further out, bringing it round, and then back down again. After about ten minutes of this, I suddenly noticed that the fly had disappeared, and that the butt of my leader pointed straight down into the water. I struck, and from deep down in the dark water, there came a silver flash as I made contact; magic! About 8 lb, he had taken the tail fly, totally without my noticing.

Because all your line is clear of the water, this method can be used to manipulate your flies around boulders that are exposed at low water in summer. Any attempt at presenting the fly in the conventional manner would simply result in getting caught up on the rocks in these conditions. Again, an upstream breeze is helpful to put a chop on the water and conceal you from the fish, as you work your flies in the streams among the rocks under your rod point, exploring each potential lie in turn. Fishing with a short line, you allow the tail fly to sink beneath the surface, but keep the dropper skating in the surface layer. Depending on the speed of the current, you can draw your flies up against the stream, swing them across, or drift them down over the lies. This gives you a variety of ways of showing your flies to any salmon that may be there.

The dragged surface fly also includes what has become known as the dry fly for salmon, although I hesitate to describe it as such. The technique is directly comparable with buzzing a sedge across the surface for trout. I was brought up to believe that dry-fly fishing meant that one's fly was fished on top of the surface of the water, without drag. If one's fly had any kind of drag or wake, it was not really dry-fly fishing. I am sure that some people will think of me as a pedantic purist to insist on such a distinction between methods, and they may well be right. However, I see it only as the difference between having one's fly stationary, or moving, relative to the water.

As a schoolboy, and later as a student, I had a number of (mostly unsuccessful) experiences with salmon on the genuine dry fly, while fishing for trout on the Don at Monymusk. I say 'mostly unsuccessful' because the salmon or, more commonly, grilse usually escaped after being hooked. A size 16 dry fly, and a 3 or 4lb leader, might be described as less than adequate for coping with a 10 or 12lb salmon.

Among my memories of these incidents is one that happened on a bright afternoon in late July 1971. I was trying the dry fly for trout in the Willowbush at Monymusk. Casting upstream, I was allowing the fly to drop down the current only about a foot out from the branches of the willows, hoping to entice one of the resident brown trout into doing something foolish.

In mid-cast, a sudden gust of wind caught my fly line, just as it was straightening above the water, and hung it on several of the branches of the willows that projected out over the river. My fly, a size 16 Badger Quill, was left dangling about a foot and a half above the surface of the water. I quietly gathered in some slack line with my left hand, and raised the rod, giving the tip a gentle twitch from time to time, to help free the line from the foliage, without snagging my fly. I had made some progress towards extracting the line from the branches, and my fly was still hanging above the surface of the water, occasionally moving in the breeze, when, to my open-mouthed astonishment, a grilse of about 6 lb leaped out of the water, seized my fly in mid-air, and fell back into the river with a splash. This was definitely more than my 4 lb leader could stand, so it promptly broke, freeing the fish after the briefest of encounters.

Had I landed that fish, it would have been the only occasion on which I could legitimately say that I had no need to even get my fly wet. It was, perhaps, the ultimate 'dry' fly presentation, as my fly had not made any contact with the surface of the water. The other point is that the incident shows just how clearly the salmon can see, and focus on objects in the air above them, through the surface of the water. It should serve as a salutary reminder to those who march about on top of the bank in broad daylight.

I have never tried to repeat the incident, by dangling a fly under my rod tip, as I suspect that the chances of consistent success with this novel form of presentation must be rather slim! However, as a freak event, I remember it well, along with other instances of salmon taking a dry fly floating naturally on the surface of the water. On many occasions on the Dee, and a few on the Don, I have seen salmon persistently taking March browns and large olives, during heavy hatches of fly, and I understand that on southern rivers like the Test, and Hampshire Avon, mayflies are frequently taken as well. I remember catching a salmon on the Don in 1977, which had positively gorged itself on March browns, to the extent that the contents of its stomach weighed nearly half a pound. Any salmon gulping down flies on a regular basis, looking for all the world like a large trout, is a ready taker, and if you fish for him with care, you should be able to catch him. I have taken such fish not just on the fly in various presentations, but on the minnow as well.

However, these examples aside, for consistent success with the dry fly, it really needs to be moving relative to the water on which it is floating; hence my preferred description of dragged surface fly, rather than dry fly. Much has been said on this subject already, by Derek Knowles in his book *Salmon on a Dry Fly*, of how, when his fly was stationary relative to the water there was no response, but as soon as it was moving, creating a little wake on the surface, up came the salmon.

It is a delightful technique, not least because of the lightness and simplicity of the tackle involved. An outfit normally used for sea trout is fine. A 10-ft single-handed rod, designed to cast a number 6 or 7 floating line, a leader tapering to 6 or 8 lb, depending on the number of rocks and your confidence, with a small selection of flies, treble hooks, and some floatant, will be all you require. The flies should be tied on fine gauge plastic tubing, in sizes ranging from $1/2$in down to $1/8$in. This last size, when combined with a size 16 treble, gives a fly with an overall length of just under $1/2$in. The flies do not need to be the famous Yellow Dolly pattern, although this shows up well on the surface of the water. A pinch of deer hair rolled around a tube, and then tied tightly in the middle so that it flares out into a ball, which can then be clipped as required, is all that I use. I like the hair to have some black fibres in it, so that it will show up well when seen from below, silhouetted against the sky. Coloured fibres of any hue mixed in with the black ones make it easy for me to see at a distance. Always dose all your dry flies with floatant before you set out, and then, if one gets waterlogged after you have hooked a fish, or for any other reason, you can change it for a fresh one without wasting any time. Also keep a close watch on your leader for any sign of abrasion, changing it regularly, and always after playing a fish.

I like to use this method on waters that I know well, so that I can guess where the fish are likely to be at any combination of water height and temperature. I also like the water to be as uncrowded with other fellow anglers as possible; ideally, and especially on a small river, to have both banks to myself. This is because I may rise a fish on one size of fly, and then spend the best part of the next hour or so trying him with different combinations of speed and size of fly, to get him to come again, and take it properly. It would be very frustrating for anyone else, waiting to fish down the pool in the conventional way, if I was clogging up the system like that. If I correctly stand aside to let the other angler fish through, as I should do, I might be worried about him disturbing the fish as he progressed down the pool. So for peace of mind, maximum solitude is best. If I am sharing the beat with someone else, I prefer them to fish the pools in front of me, so that I can leave half an hour or so for any fish to settle before trying myself, and thereby not having to worry about getting in anyone's way.

The essence of the technique is to cast your fly beyond the fish, and then to draw it slowly back across them, so that it leaves a small wake on the surface. Because of the need for accuracy, and to be able to see your fly clearly at all times, the typical cast is unlikely to be much more than about twenty yards, so pay attention to concealing yourself from the fish. Your cast can be either up and across, or down and across, depending on the individual lie, and the best line of approach to it. The direction and strength of the wind may also be a factor. As this is usually a low water technique for me, when the flow may be very gentle, I prefer to have a bit of an upstream breeze which helps to ripple the water.

If you are casting down and across in a pool with even quite a modest flow through it, you may not need to use much hand-lining to get your fly to drag nicely on the surface. Casting upstream in the same place, and you will need to raise your rod gently, pulling in line with your free hand at the same time, to achieve the correct presentation. With the small flies I have mentioned, water temperatures need to be fairly high, certainly into the upper 50sF and above.

The technique will work at lower temperatures than this, but unless the water is slow moving (and the speed of your fly relative to it), you are going to need much larger flies. This in turn will mean heavier rods and lines to cast them, and the delicacy of the method, and therefore much of its charm, will be lost. Just as salmon will take a big streamer or long wing fly riffling the surface when the water temperature is in the mid-40sF, I see no reason why they would not take a 'dry' fly doing exactly the same thing at that temperature. I have not tried to find out, because I have never tied any dry flies large enough. If I did, I suspect some of my less polite friends would christen the flies 'Floating Hedgehogs' to go with my Drowned Mice. It might be fun to try, because using a bushy dry fly more than 2in long would certainly wake up all the fish in the pool.

When water temperatures are in the low 60sF, my standard fly sizes are tied on $3/8$in or $1/4$in tubes, with the tiny $1/8$in usually reserved for gently drifting across slow water. However, there is no rigid scale of sizes of fly for any particular water temperature, because so much will depend on how fast you drag your fly across the surface. Many times salmon will rise to your fly, but without actually taking it into their mouths. This is usually because the fly is too large in relation to the speed at which it is being fished for the particular water temperature. The stock response to a fish which rises to a fly, but 'misses', is to try him with a size smaller fly presented in the same way. As an alternative, you can try him with the same fly, but fished significantly quicker. You can also try him with a larger fly fished so fast that it positively bounces back across the surface towards you. After doing that, have another go with your original combination, as then you may well get a positive take. The permutations in this game are nearly infinite, and it is easy to spend the best part of a morning engrossed in a single fish that rises regularly to your different offerings, but refuses to take hold. When fishing at Anne's Seat on the Don at Monymusk, I once rose the same fish nine times without his touching the fly, before a carelessly bungled cast caught the bank, and I disturbed him while trying to release the hook. He would not come again after that.

It is an enthralling branch of flyfishing, and I can think of few better ways to pass a late summer afternoon, especially if there are reports of the odd grilse being around after a small spate a week or so before. Because of the lightness of the tackle, and the very small hooks used, it is not really a suitable method for large fish, which normally manage to get away. With fresh fish, tiny trebles will not usually have a deep enough purchase to prevent their tearing free during a prolonged struggle. Coloured fish have tougher mouths, and therefore tend to stay on the hook longer. Whether you use a large streamer fly in cold water, dibble a medium-size fly from your dropper at intermediate temperatures, or draw a tiny dry fly slowly over the surface of a gentle, summer-warmed stream, the dragged surface fly represents a useful variation in technique on classic floating line fishing. If you know a pool has fish in it, and they have been slow to respond to the conventional approach, try the dragged surface fly in any of its guises, as a suitably radical alternative. Success will stimulate your ambition to explore its wider possibilities, and you may end up in the company of those whose mastery is such that they seldom use any other method.

Section 5: The Nymph

Inspired by the chapter 'Experiments with Salmon', in Frank Sawyer's book *Nymphs and the Trout*, I tried to repeat his tactics on the Don. I reasoned that if they worked in Hampshire, they should also work in Aberdeenshire. I tried out the technique on a small red fish (later returned to the river), that had been lying in full view under the broken parapet above the bridge at Monymusk for several months. My prompt success with a little black and yellow tube convinced me that this was a significant addition to my array of low water tactics. It has now become one of my favourite methods in the warm water and reduced flows of summer and early autumn. Typically, if I fish down the pools in the morning with conventional floating line tactics, or a dragged surface fly, on my return upstream I will search selected hot spots, and anywhere that I have seen a fish, with the nymph.

I had a long apprenticeship with the nymph, which caught me many brown trout during my summer holidays as a schoolboy and student. I found it particularly useful as a means of extracting trout from backwaters, where often there would be two or three cruising around, feeding among the patches of froth and the other debris that tends to revolve gently on the surface in such places. Because of the circulating current in a backwater, presenting a conventional dry fly without drag is often difficult, and an ordinary wet fly was all too often ignored. However, a pheasant tail nymph, cast from across the river into a backwater, and allowed to sink, would be grabbed by a trout, just as the current caught the line, and started to drag the nymph out into the main stream, lifting the fly in the water as it did so. Casting into the backwater from across the river helped reduce the problems of concealment and disturbance, but the crucial factor in inducing the trout to take, was the rising path of the nymph through the water.

I use exactly this technique when fishing for salmon in Anne's Seat at Monymusk on the Don. Towards the lower end of the pool, on the south bank, a large point juts out into the river. Parallel with, and below this point runs a deep channel. (In the late 1970s I explored this in a wet suit, and at the time I reckoned it to be about 18 ft deep.) In low water, there is only the gentlest of currents down this channel. Behind the point on the south bank, is a backwater adjacent to the deep channel.

This channel provides a good long-term holding lie for resident fish in low water. Because of its depth and the slow current, it is not usually thought of as being good taking water for the fly. However, I found that by casting my flies into the backwater, from the north bank, and allowing them to sink, when the gentle stream in the deep channel bellied my line downstream, it would draw them back up in the water, and this was often enough to persuade a fish to take. Sometimes a little hand lining was needed to assist the process.

The principal is to allow your nymph to sink deeply in the water, ideally to about the same level as the fish, and then, as it approaches the salmon, it should be made to rise up in the water. This calls for accurate knowledge of the precise (or likely) position of the fish. It is not a technique that I use to search large areas of water. Ideally, I like to be able to see the salmon that I am fishing for in its lie, and if that is not possible, to know the exact location of where it ought to be. Since I usually try to start the nymph on its upward journey when it is about a yard or so in front of the salmon, accurate positioning of the fly is important, and this means short casting, typically 15–20 yards. The light, single-handed rod is ideal for the purpose.

Grease the butt of your leader (which should taper to about 8 lb), so that it will float on the surface of the water. Just as in trout fishing, you should watch this carefully. Any check, or drawing under of the leader, should be tightened into at once. Remember to adjust the length of the leader to the depth of water you are fishing. You will need a much longer leader to get your fly down properly, in 14 or 15 ft of water, than in 4 or 5 ft. In low water, the salmon may have congregated for security in the only really deep holding pools on the beat. To fish these, I will use a leader that may be more than 20 ft long. In shallow water I may only need one that is 9 or 10 ft in length.

When fishing deep water, you must also allow more time for your fly to sink (taking your leader down with it), which means casting further upstream of the fish than in shallow water. This will also be affected by the speed of the current. Again, in faster water, you will need to cast further upstream of the fish than you do in slow water.

It is not always essential to sink your fly right down to the level of the fish. Sometimes I use what can best be described as mid-water nymphing, or sink and draw tactics. Usually when casting downstream, but it can also be done when casting upstream, I allow the fly to drift down for a few yards, sinking several feet into the water as it does so. I then draw it up in the water by pulling in some line and raising the rod tip. I then release slack line and lower the rod tip again, allowing the nymph to sink once more. A few yards lower down the pool, I will again draw it up in the water. The process can be repeated, so that the fly is drawn up in the water several times during the fishing of a single cast. If you are not sure of the exact positions of the fish, this enables one to cover far more water than the true nymph-style approach. It also works well enough to serve as a useful introduction to the technique, and has the virtue that it often induces very positive takes from the fish.

Flies do not need to be traditional nymph patterns. I normally use a Hairy Mary tied directly onto a small treble, but I don't think the pattern matters at all. It is the way the fly moves through the water that is important. Normal sizes of treble hooks are from 8 to 14. I no longer bother to use those with a specially long shank. To help the fly sink, a few turns of lead wire under the dressing of the body is an advantage. Alternatively you can use a heavyweight treble such as

Partridge's 'Rob Wilson XX Strong Outpoint Treble', although the smallest size currently available is a size 10. The thicker metal of these has another advantage in that it does not tear through the flesh of the fish so readily as the fine wire of ordinary small trebles.

The fly can be presented to the fish from either above or below. Casting from below the fish aids concealment, which is important when you are fishing such a short line. If you cast upstream, gather in the slack line as it floats down towards you, and then as your fly reaches a point immediately in front of where you think the salmon is, gently raise your rod point. At the same time, you should pull in some line with your spare hand. This will cause your nymph to be drawn up in the water as it passes over the fish. Always try several casts in the same place, as the salmon may not respond to your first attempt, but only after your third or fourth presentation. Let your fly drift a good way downstream of the fish before you lift off and re-cast. Not only will this reduce the risk of disturbance, but salmon will sometimes turn and take the fly only after it has passed, and is a couple of yards downstream behind them.

When you are casting downstream towards the fish, which is usually only practical in a fairly gentle stream, you must have plenty of loose line floating slack, on the surface; otherwise your nymph will not sink down to the level of the fish, but will behave more like the conventional fly on the floating line. You can help create the slack by making your forward cast too vigorous, and then checking your line in mid-air, so that it falls like a snake across the water. You may also wish to shake some additional line loose from your rod tip. Provided your line stays absolutely loose and slack on the surface, so that the current can not draw it taut, your fly will sink. When it reaches the desired position, raise your rod point slightly, and draw in sufficient line to halt the downstream progress of your fly. Buoyed by the current and the tightened line, your fly will swing up in the water to rise attractively in front of, and over, the nose of the fish. The speed of the water, and how much slack line you have floating on it, will determine the amount of line you need to draw in.

These are very similar tactics to those employed to create an induced take, when fishing with a nymph for brown trout, and there is much to recommend them in low water conditions. When fishing a calm pool with only the gentlest of flows, your fly and line can enter the water far enough upstream not to disturb a fish, and then drift slowly down to it. As it is deeply sunk, your leader can neither glitter nor throw a shadow to cause alarm in bright sunlight and low water. You can experiment with different speeds of lift to try and trigger a taking response. If you pay sufficient attention to stealth and concealment, you will find that nymph tactics create a most useful extra string to your bow when conditions for conventional salmon fly fishing are described as hopeless.

Part 4 — Persistence

Together with preparation and presentation, persistence is essential to the success of the salmon angler. The determination needed to keep fishing when others have given up will be rewarded, as the following incident shows.

It is around four o'clock in the afternoon of Tuesday 4 September 1984, and I am standing on the cauld, at the bottom of the Temple Pool of The Lees fishings, at Coldstream on the Tweed. The drought which has lasted since early spring has yet to break on Tweedside. The river is very low, and warm. Blanket weed has grown over large areas of the bottom of the river, and pieces continually break off to float downstream. The water is like a rather unpleasant green vegetable soup. There is a pervasive, canal-like stench from the rotting weed.

Conventional flyfishing for salmon is well nigh impossible, as the fly collects a lump of blanket weed within a second or two of entering the water at every cast. It is hot, and the sun blazes down from a blue sky.

The other rod who was fishing the beat with me, packed up after lunch, and left for home in the south, having decided that there was no chance of a fish this week. The third member of our party, on hearing of the state of the river, decided not to bother to make the journey up from London.

I am casting a $1\frac{1}{2}$in metal Devon minnow about twenty yards upstream, and reeling it in fast downstream towards myself. Sometimes I can make it travel a few yards down the pool before it collects a lump of weed. I have been doing this for over two hours now, and have long since given up any thought of concealing myself by keeping low, and standing on the downstream side of the concrete cauld. I can see five salmon lying on the shingle bottom of the river in front of me, just where the current starts to speed up before it pours through the slap in the cauld to my right. Both gillies are sitting beside me on the concrete. We talk about salmon, and salmon fishing; life, the universe, and everything, as we have done all afternoon. There hasn't been a fish off the beat for months, and all three of us are convinced that conditions are hopeless.

I continue casting the minnow upsteam, retrieving it downstream, over or past one side or other of each of the fish, more or less in turn. It is an uninspiring, and rather monotonous way of fishing. I am becoming very bored with having to remove weed from the minnow and swivel every cast.

I am not even looking at the minnow, when without any warning, one of the fish takes it firmly. Thump! Thump! And the rod bends into him. He's on! I turn to the gillies and say quietly, 'Got one!' Both gillies give me the kind of look that schoolmasters reserve for small boys who make remarks of particular stupidity. I nod my head and repeat 'I've got one on.' I can see that one of the gillies is opening his mouth to say 'No, it's just the bottom', when the fish suddenly leaps clear of the water, and the look of scorn is replaced first by shocked disbelief, and then by panic an instant later. 'It's a fish! Get the net! Get the net! Don't lose him! Oh, don't lose him, sir!'

A few minutes later, a slightly stale, but still keepable fish of a little over eight pounds, is safely in the net. There is a lot of good-natured joking, and banter between the three of us. We are all very pleased.

This shows the importance of persistence in successful salmon fishing. I had been casting over the same group of fish for well over two hours without a pause. Normally I am a great believer in the importance of concealment, but on this occasion I had been standing there and making the same movements for so long that I think that the fish had grown accustomed to my presence, and no longer considered me a threat. I do not know why one of the fish should have chosen to respond to the lure at that moment, having already seen it, and ignored it, literally hundreds of times previously that afternoon. However, incidents of this nature, where I have fished hard over a known group of fish, and where, eventually, one has taken the lure, have been too common to be ignored. If the fish are there, and you carry on doing the right thing for long enough, something will drop in the end.

I finished the week with a total of six fish despite the adverse conditions, which ensured that many beats remained unfished. Although my gillies carried out an extensive research operation (which included visiting a number of hostelries in Coldstream and Kelso on the Friday evening!), they heard no reports of any other salmon being caught. If you don't fish you won't catch anything. There is always a chance of success if you do.

Some of my most frustrating fishing experiences have happened on the Don at Monymusk, where, on more than one occasion, I have only been able to find a single fish in the entire beat, which I then pursued exclusively, sometimes flogging away for hours in the day, sometimes leaving it alone apart from a few very careful casts at dawn or dusk. After days, and sometimes weeks of this war of attrition, I have finally had the fish take my fly, only to lose it. When the loss has been due to my own stupidity, or lack of concentration, it has added insult to the injury to my pride. `All that effort for nothing' was my feeling at the time. However, in retrospect, this is not the case. I was doing the right thing, and kept at it, and in the end succeeded in getting the fish to take, thus proving that my tactics were right. Lack of concentration, or over-anxiety, can always be overcome in the future with a bit of will-power, self-confidence, and self-discipline.

Persistence also means sustaining one's concentration and motivation. With every cast, the angler should think, 'How is my fly fishing?' And try to imagine it. Is the fly moving as it should, or, for instance, is it being dragged too rapidly over the lies by the current? Is it deep enough in the water? Thoughts such as these should occupy the angler's mind all the time that his fly is fishing. If the angler's mind wanders, perhaps distracted by the beauty of his surroundings, or by animals or birds near him, or worse still by thoughts about problems at home or in the office, his catch will be only a fraction of what it would have been had his concentration been sustained.

It is all too easy for fishing to become a mechanical process, with each cast thoughtlessly repeating the last, while the angler seems in a hurry to reach the tail of the pool and to finish. This is especially likely when the pool is a long, and superficially, a relatively featureless glide, with a nasty wind blowing from across the river to make casting difficult. The necessarily deep, and prolonged wading is a chill business in the cold water of the early part of the season. In such a pool, perhaps a quarter of a mile long, it is easy to see why anglers are often in a hurry to get out of the water. However, if he is well-insulated against the cold of both air and water, he is much more likely to be able to concentrate on both casting, and fishing his fly properly, resulting in a substantial increase in the probability of success. Having the proper clothing, from the soles of your waders upwards, is of crucial importance in terms of improving your productive fishing time, and your ability to be persistent.

I have seen many people who happily spend several hundred pounds (or more) on a week's fishing, and nearly as much on their hotel bill and yet are unwilling to spend a hundred pounds or so on replacing their waders once every three or four years. Deep wading in a pair of leaky waders in February or March is unlikely to prolong your fishing life, or to add to your pleasure in the sport, unless you have very strange tastes indeed! Similarly, some people will use the same fishing jacket year after year. After twenty years' wear the jacket will not be waterproof, and its lining will have lost much of its ability to insulate against the cold. In cold, wet weather, the wearer will also be cold and wet; he will also be more likely to take an extended lunch hour in the fishing hut, and to return early in the evening because of the miserable weather. This has a dramatic effect in reducing productive fishing time.

This is best shown by the story of two salmon fishers, whom I shall call Kermit and Miss Piggy, who find that a spell of bad weather coincides with their fishing in Scotland in early March.

It is not a pleasant day to be fishing. The river is being lashed by cold, hard, sleety rain, driven by a northwesterly wind. On the higher ground heavy snow will be falling, so the river is unlikely to rise much during the day. Kermit and Miss Piggy arrive at the fishing hut on the beat at 9 a.m. Kermit is well-equipped for the conditions, having a waterproof outer coat with a hood attached, a sound pair of chest waders, gloves, mitts, scarf, and plenty of insulation in the form of thermal pile trousers and jacket. He is dressed and fishing by half past nine.

However, Miss Piggy is in no hurry, as she doesn't like the look of the weather, and potters about the fishing hut for a while, before starting to fish at 10 a.m.. She is less well wrapped up than her colleague. Her old fishing jacket combined with an extra sweater is neither as warm nor as waterproof as Kermit's newer and more suitable clothing. She doesn't wear a hood, and her woollen mitts are rather frayed. It doesn't take the rain and sleet long to find the gap between her cloth cap and her collar, so her head and neck are soon cold and wet, as are her hands, encased in sodden mitts. After a couple of hours, she is wet through, and very cold. She can scarcely feel a thing through her numbed fingers. She is impatient to finish the pool, and to get back to the hut for lunch, and a dram or two by the warmth of the fire. The combination of the cold, the wind, her numb hands, and her impatience, is adversely affecting her casting. When she doesn't bungle the cast entirely, she is scarcely reaching three-quarters of her normal casting length across the pool. Also, in her hurry to finish the pool, she isn't allowing her cast to fish out properly, and she wades five or six paces downstream between each cast, rather than her normal one or two steps. No one could describe her progress as the patient, methodical search of the water that is needed to find an early season fish. She is not fishing effectively. She returns to the warmth of the hut at half past twelve, having fished effectively for less than two hours, despite being out for two and a half.

By contrast, Kermit is still warm and dry. He is consequently able to continue to concentrate on his casting, and on fishing his fly properly. He stops for lunch at one o'clock, having fished effectively for almost all the three and a half hours that he has been on the river. As he can drive his car to the next pool that he intends to fish, he decides not to return to the hut, but to eat his sandwiches in the car while watching the river. It takes about twenty minutes to eat them, and whilst he does so, a salmon shows twice, with the distinctive splosh of a resident fish, about two-thirds of the way down the pool. 'Hallo! Hallo!' he thinks, and mentally marks the spot down for particularly close attention. He is fishing the pool with renewed interest by half past one. He continues through the afternoon, stopping at around half past five, and returns to the hut for a rest, and to find out how Miss Piggy has fared.

There is a note on the hut table telling him that she has packed up for the day, and looks forward to seeing him in the hotel bar before supper. Kermit eats an orange left over from his picnic lunch. Then, feeling rested and refreshed, as he avoided getting cold and wet during the day, decides to fish for a final hour or so as the light fades. With the approach of evening, the wind drops, and the stormy conditions of the day abate. He again starts with renewed optimism, and continues to fish till half past seven, when he packs up.

Miss Piggy, on the other hand, didn't leave the hut till nearly a quarter to three in the afternoon, having enjoyed a large drink, and a long chat with the gillie. However, out in the cold and wet, the warmth of the hut and the drink is soon lost. By quarter past four she is again chilled to the bone, and has had enough for one day. She packs up, telling the gillie that 'all salmon fishers must be mad if they say they enjoy their sport on a day like today'. The gillie, with his eye on a supply of whisky for the week, and on his tip at the end of it, doesn't disagree. She has fished effectively for about three out of the four hours she spent on the water, with an additional three hours in the hut.

However, Kermit has fished effectively all day, losing only half an hour's preparation time in the morning, half an hour for lunch, and half an hour in the late afternoon. His effective fishing time totals some nine hours throughout the day. If all other factors are equal, Kermit is three times as likely to land a salmon as Miss Piggy, simply because he had the right clothing to enable him to persist with his fishing despite the conditions. If the bad weather continues throughout the week, the odds will become even more heavily stacked in favour of Kermit, as Miss Piggy will find her self-confidence dwindling. With Kermit spending more time fishing, his knowledge of the beat will grow faster than Miss Piggy's, and he will also be catching more fish. This in turn will reinforce the acceleration of his learning curve, because each fish successfully landed confirms that the correct tactics were employed, and provides a basis on which to work the next time he fishes the pool. Kermit will therefore become increasingly likely to adopt the correct approach to fishing any pool on the beat, and so his success will feed on itself.

Poor Miss Piggy. Not only is she having to cope with the foul weather, and is struggling to find a fish, but Kermit, whom she thinks of as an angler of similar ability to herself, is steadily finding a fish or two most days. A tinge of jealousy and self-doubt soon creeps in, and Miss Piggy thinks she must be doing something wrong. She begins to try wild variations in tactics as her desperation increases, thus reducing her chances still further. She becomes worried about her lack of success, which stops her thinking about how her fly is fishing. This means that her fishing becomes a mechanical exercise, with her mind elsewhere. If a fish does take, she will probably lose it through over-anxiety. And so her confidence will deteriorate further. The whole rotten process starting because she thought that she could get by without buying the proper clothing to cope with the conditions. Sadly, too few anglers learn from their mistakes, which, so often, are rooted in something as simple as the tale of Kermit and Miss Piggy.

I know several people whose only fishing (and shooting) jackets date from the 1960s, and some who insist that a tweed jacket and cloth cap are all that is needed by way of protective clothing for salmon fishing. I have even met one man who thinks that to don an additional heavy oiled wool sweater is sufficient, when he is wearing chest waders. I remarked on this once, and he replied, 'if it rains, I get wet. But I find that a jacket interferes with my freedom of movement.' I raised an eyebrow, and commented, 'so will rigor mortis!' He thought I was joking. If you are properly clad you will fish longer, and catch more salmon, than those who are not.

In the tale of Kermit and Miss Piggy, rather than return to the hut, Kermit consumed his sandwiches in the car overlooking the river. This is an important way to save time during the fishing day. There are those who think that I am unsociable because I don't like to return to the main hut, or worse still, the local hostelry, for lunch. Not so, I am simply looking after my valuable fishing turns. If I return to the hut, the whole process, from stopping fishing, travelling back to the hut, taking off waders and jackets, having a drink, eating lunch and chatting to my fellow anglers, putting on waders and jackets again, travelling back to the pool and restarting fishing, seems to take about an hour and a half, or even longer. If I eat my sandwiches on the bank of the next pool that I plan to fish, (or in the car if the weather is bad), the whole process will take a maximum of half an hour, and I will have gained an hour's fishing time. Over the course of a week, I will have gained an extra six hours fishing time over my friends who return to the hut for their more leisurely luncheon each day. Six hours can easily mean an extra, or indeed, the only fish or two for the week.

On the subject of lunch, I don't think that alcohol and serious salmon fishing really mix. Some people think that a large hip flask is an essential item of tackle. I do not. I have a tin of beer with my sandwiches at lunch-time, and that is all. Any more, and I notice that my casting and fishing judgement is impaired. Alcohol does not help my wading either. Most salmon fishers only have a week or two each year to pursue their sport. If their sport is important to them, they should concentrate on it when they have their brief opportunity to do so, and leave the wining, dining, and entertaining of their friends to the rest of the year. On a fishing holiday, the proper time and place for a sociable drink is at home, or in the hotel bar, after the day's fishing is over.

The other advantage of eating my sandwiches on the bank of the next pool that I intend to fish, is that so often, while enjoying the opportunity for a good long look at the pool, I see something important or interesting. It may be a fish showing, in which case I can mark the spot for later attention, or even a run of fish entering the pool, in which case I can (temporarily!) abandon my sandwiches and grab the fly rod for immediate action. I may notice something about the way that the current enters, or flows through the pool, that will help me to fish it better. Or I may detect the first signs of a change in weather conditions or the state of the water, which might be useful in deciding tactics for the afternoon. Or it may be a spectacular piece of natural drama. For instance, on two or three occasions one year, while eating my sandwiches beside the Top Gannet at Ballogie on the Dee, I watched a sparrow-hawk chasing swallows across the river. I never saw it catch one, but the high speed pursuit of split second turns, as the birds flashed after each other across the pool, towards the trees growing on the rocky face of the far bank, was breathtakingly thrilling to watch. It is unlikely that I would see anything so wonderful from the comfort of the inside of a fishing hut.

Another way of improving effective fishing time, particularly when water temperatures are in the middle to upper 40sF, and you may wish to switch from sunk line to floating line and back again repeatedly throughout the day, is to carry more than one fly rod. The process of removing a fly, (or two flies if a dropper is involved), putting it in the appropriate fly box, taking the reel off the rod and putting it into its case and into the bag, getting the new reel out of the bag and on to the rod, and the line threaded properly through the rings, a new fly out of its box, and tied on to the leader, and the box put away in the bag, all takes time, certainly several minutes. On some occasions, you may have to repeat this process ten or more times in a single day. Clearly you would gain an hour's effective fishing time if all you had to do was to reel in, put down the rod you are using, pick up the second rod, lying ready for use, and resume casting. Again, over the course of a week's fishing, this could improve your effective fishing time by several hours, with obvious consequences for your chances of successfully catching a salmon.

Another problem of using the same rod all the time, is that because changing lines is a chore, the temptation is not to bother. This could cost you a fish on any one day, and possibly several fish in a week, if you succumb to temptation. One of my salmon fishing rules is, 'always take the trouble', and it is especially applicable in these circumstances. To avoid that temptation, when water temperatures are in the mid 40sF, I will usually carry three fly rods, one set up with a floating line, and two set up with different weights of sinking line.

Persistence in salmon fishing also means making sure that your fly is in the water at the most productive times of the day (or night!). In the early part of the season, this will be around the middle of the day, just as the water temperature rises that crucial half-degree or so. This accounts for many of the salmon hooked just as the fisher himself was about to stop for lunch. This also underlines my dislike of beats where there is either a lunch-time changeover of the sections or pools that each rod has to fish, or, worse still, all rods must be off the water for an hour between one and two. This latter rule usually dates from the day when every rod was accompanied by a personal gillie, and was designed to ensure that the gillie got a lunch-hour too.

In the early part of the season, in the absence of a heavy overnight frost, there is no reason why the morning should not be productive. I have often hooked a fish within a few minutes of starting, and long before the other rods have arrived at the beat. I always like to fish in the evening, even in the early part of the season, although a hard frost as the sun sets will not help matters. (When your line is continually freezing in the rod rings, and your reel seizes up, it is time to stop anyway!) In the absence of severe frost, the evening may well produce your only fish of the day. I can remember clearly a week on the Dee in February, when all my fish were caught after 5 p.m., and the other rods, and the gillies, had finished for the day. They were also the only fish caught on the beat that week. So if you can, fish on into the evening.

As the days lengthen into April and May, the evening session becomes of crucial importance, but the best taking times during each day will be dominated by the way the water temperature fluctuates. For instance, if there has been a sharp fall in water temperature overnight, it is less likely that there will be much activity before ten or eleven o'clock in the morning, with the best prospects being from lunch-time onwards. However, if temperatures overnight are stable, a prompt start in the morning may find a group of fish in the pool that would have moved on upstream if left till later in the day. But, whatever happens, make sure you fish the evening session for that brief hour or two of magic as the light fades into darkness.

Salmon do take in the dark, but generally I, and most other people that I know, don't bother to fish for them at that time. Trying to scramble up a steep bank out of the water, and then to pursue an active fish along the bank through the boulders and pot-holes is not my idea of fun on a dark night. The risk of personal injury, and of damage to tackle is too high. In any case, burning the candle at both ends, by fishing both during the day and the night, will certainly lead to your becoming over-tired, even if you do suffer from insomnia. If you are over-tired, your concentration will suffer, reducing your ability to control your fly properly, and thus decreasing your chances of catching a fish; so a balanced approach to the hours that you fish is best, and the advice, 'don't overdo it', is sound.

In June and early July, when it never gets really dark in northern Scotland, the weather will again influence your tactics in terms of the hours that you fish. During a heatwave, with the sun shining down from the merciless glare of a bright sky, the best prospects for fishing may well be from nine or ten p.m. through till five or six a.m. and you can enjoy a large breakfast and a heavy lunch, and sleep through the heat of the day. (Don't blame me if your friends wonder why you have not got a sun tan!) I love being out in the gentle light of the early summer morning, as I see so much wildlife quietly going about its business, before humans get up to disturb the peace. Otters, deer, badgers and foxes are all on the move in the early morning. I remember an otter surfacing four or five feet from me, under the middle joint of the old 11 ft Sharpe's Aberdeen that I was using, as I waded down a pool on the Don early one morning. He looked at me with his large brown eyes for several seconds, before sliding silently underwater to disappear once more.

If, however, the weather is cool and wet, daytime fishing in June or July can be just as productive as at any other time of the year. Again, try to fish either the early morning, or the evening periods, in addition to your daytime fishing. Don't try to fish both overnight and through the day as well.

As the days shorten, and the weather cools, through the months from August to November, the warming of the water temperature around midday grows in importance again. On a chill November morning on the Tweed, after a sharp overnight frost, there may not be much moving till the air has warmed appreciably, and that may not be till after 10 or 11 a.m. However, just as in the early season, it is wise to carry on fishing into the evening, even though your best chances of success will be during the middle of the day.

Persistence in salmon fishing involves several different principles which can be summarized as follows:

1   Don't give up. No matter how hopeless the conditions, keep trying. If your fly is out of the water, it won't catch many fish! Success under bad conditions will give you far greater satisfaction, and will teach you more about salmon, and salmon fishing, than will success when conditions are easy.
2   Don't let your fishing become a mechanical exercise. Always think about how your fly is fishing, especially about its depth, and its speed of movement relative to the water and the fish. If you are not happy with the way that it is fishing, think of some ploy that might improve things. Maintain your concentration at all times.
3   Maximize your productive fishing time, so that as little as possible of the time that you have available to spend by the water is wasted.
4   Invest in the proper clothing, so that you can carry on fishing in comfort in the worst of weather.
5   Always try to fish as the light fades in the evening, no matter how foul the weather during the day.
6   Don't overdo it. Spending too long on the water may lead to fatigue, which will lessen your efficiency as an angler, and thereby actually reduce your chances of success. (In any case, wading while you are tired is much more likely to lead to an early bath than wading when concentration, strength, co-ordination and reflexes are in better shape.)

Some of this chapter's advice may sound too much like hard work for some people. However, success in any sport requires hard work. Those who are not prepared to make the effort should not criticize, or be jealous of those who are. My brief holidays became very important during my stress-filled years pretending to be a stockbroker, and the only way that I could relax and forget the worries of the office, was to concentrate totally on my fishing whilst on holiday. I then found that the more effort I put into my fishing, the more enjoyment I got out of it. The more I enjoyed my fishing, the less I worried about work, and the more relaxed and happy I became. Those who put less effort into succeeding at their sport also get less pleasure out of it.

Water conditions

Top: The Willowbush at Monymusk on the Don. The quiet water in the foreground is where the salmon fell through the net (page 13, Tackle). A grilse seized the fly here in mid-air when the line was caught up in the willows on the far bank (page 87, Dragged Surface Fly).

Bottom: September on the Tay at Taymount. At this height the fish lie in the quieter water plainly visible beside the main stream.

Water conditions

Top: The author fishing Rurholm on the Vosso. Fish forcing their way up the rapids pull into the quieter water behind the groynes for a brief rest.

Bottom: Top Gannet, Ballogie, River Dee. Although the drop-off is now only a gentle slope, salmon still lie in the depths, which show dark beyond the shelf of yellow shingle.

Proof of success

Four salmon, three sea trout and one grilse on the floating line. Note how the grilse (bottom), with slim pointed head and more deeply forked tail, fewer spots etc., differs from the three sea trout with their blunter, rounded heads, squarer tails and more numerous spots.

Hooking the fish

Top: "Right in the scissors". The author unhooks a 15½lb salmon from the Naver, taken with the floating line and ½″ Hairy Mary tube on the dropper. The treble hook is just visible in the very corner of the fish's mouth.

Bottom: The floating line and ½″ Hairy Mary tube also accounted for these two salmon and one sea trout from the Dee in May 1991.

Part 5 — The Take and After

Section 1: Hooking the Fish

Twelfth May 1984. It is very bright, with a cloudless sky, and a hard, dazzling glitter from the sun on the water. There was a frost overnight, and although this has now cleared, the east wind blowing up the river still has a chilly bite to it. I am fishing the Lower Flats at Ballogie on the Dee.

Towards the tail of the pool is a large submerged rock which, at that time, created a favourite temporary resting place for salmon in the eddy behind it, after they had swum up through the rapids immediately above the Spout and the Pot. I am fishing with a 16-ft carbon rod, a floating line, and two half-inch Hairy Mary tubes. I have waded in till I am a little more than knee deep, and am casting only a modest distance, perhaps twenty-five yards. With plenty of mending, I allow my fly to swing slowly across the main current till it reaches the edge of the eddy behind the rock, and then to drop gently downstream, along a path between the current and the eddy.

When my fly reaches a point some three yards below the rock, there is a small, splashy rise. Watching, I wait for my line to move before I tighten into the fish. To my surprise nothing happens. I let my fly drift further down before it swings across the eddy. Having re-cast, my fly follows the same path, but there is no response. Again I cast, and again my fly drifts between the main current and the outside edge of the eddy. This time there is a small, splashy rise, but disappointingly, my line again remains undisturbed, without the hoped for draw of a fish pulling it under and away.

Puzzled, I strip the line in, remove the tail fly, and in its place I tie on a slightly smaller ($^3/_8$in) tube of the same pattern. I re-cast, and drift my fly down the same line over the fish, but nothing happens. I repeat this several times without response, before deciding that on this occasion, the smaller fly is not the correct solution.

I remove it and re-attach the original $^1/_2$in tube, to try again. This time there is the now familiar small splashy rise, but once more the line does not move. So I decide to see whether presenting my fly in a different way will make the fish take more positively. I try all the permutations of changing the speed at which my fly moves, and the angle at which it travels across the lie, without response. These range from holding the fly on the dangle, so that it hangs stationary above the fish, to putting a downstream mend into the line and moving my rod point round inshore to drag the fly at speed over the fish. I return to drifting the fly down the edge of the current, and again the fish responds with a small splashy rise, but without moving the line. This is the fourth time it has risen, and so far I have neither felt nor seen the slightest indication that it has made contact with the fly.

I try a size larger ($^5/_8$in) tube in place of the existing $^1/_2$in tail fly, but without response. Nothing happens either when I present it at different angles and speeds. So, once more I revert to my original $^1/_2$in tube and allow it to slide slowly downstream over the fish as before. Yet again, there is the same small splashy rise that does not connect, and it is repeated a few casts later, which makes it the sixth time the fish has risen. I pause for a minute or two, in order to try to work out what to do next.

Mentally, I replay the sight of each rise as it happened, examining my memory for clues. Then an idea begins to form, and the more I think about it, the stronger the conviction grows. I am nearly sure that in the last two rises there may have been the tiniest hesitation in the movement of the end of the line as it drifted down. Quite suddenly I see clearly what has been happening. The fish, with great delicacy, has been playing with my fly. At each rise it has sucked the fly in, then blown it out again, without closing its mouth on it. Once the nature of the problem is known, the solution is easy to find. I will have to strike at the first indication of a rise.

The strike will have to be quick, very quick. It will also have to be upwards, with the intention of hooking the fish in the top lip or the roof of its mouth. A sideways strike will simply remove the fly from between the open jaws. I cannot present the fly properly from below, unfortunately, as this would be much the best way, with the fly being drawn back into the mouth of the fish on the strike. I will need to move downstream, nearer to the fish, to shorten the line. This will produce a steeper angle when I raise the rod, and so improve the chances of successfully hooking the fish in the upper part of its mouth.

With quiet care not to make any splash, nor to scrape any rocks, I wade very softly down the stream for several yards, and strip in a similar amount of line. Gently I cast the short line across the current, fish it round, and allow the flies to slip down slowly between the edge of stream and the eddy behind the rock. I hold the rod firmly with both hands, the line tightly pressed against the butt by my forefinger, and I stand poised, ready to respond instantly.

The water humps into the familiar form of the small, splashy rise. As it does, I bring the rod flashing back, with all the speed that the leverage of both hands can create. Half-way through the stroke it stops dead. For an awful second I am sure it is going to break under the strain between the driving force of the upward sweep of my arms, and the rocklike immobility of the far end of the line.

For a moment it feels as though I have indeed hooked a rock. 'But it can't be, there aren't any rocks there', I think, as relief floods through me that I have not broken my rod, which is still bent over, with the taut line and leader steeply angled into the water. After two or three seconds, the 'rock' suddenly starts to move, very slowly, pulling the rod down. It's a fish!

It feels very solid, very heavy. I have the feeling that it does not really know what is happening, that it is unaware that it is hooked, yet. It leans against the rod with a gradually increasing pull, dragging the point down steadily. I do not let it take any line, and it stops, holding stationary in the water. Slowly I raise the rod, till the butt is once more pointing up at an angle of a bit more than 45°, and the fish drifts a yard or so towards me.

With a firm grasp of rod and line, I begin to wade carefully inshore, and diagonally upstream. Steadily I make progress, drawing the fish up after me. Any fish that I hook in the Lower Flat I like to walk upstream for over 100 yards, till he is safely in the Upper Flat, where I can play him, away from the risk of his making a dash downstream, over the Spout and into the Pot.

I have nearly reached the shore now, and slowly, ponderously, the fish is following, as I firmly but quietly lead it upstream. A few more side-steps and I will be on the bank. The fish stops in the water and leans against the rod, but I don't let any line out, and soon I can re-start my upstream progress. The fish follows for a few yards, and I am on the bank. Then it stops and leans against the rod. As before I don't allow it to take out any line, and after a few seconds I can move upstream again.

I have only taken another couple of side-steps up along the edge of the bank, with the fish obediently following, when, suddenly, I feel the fly pull out of its mouth, and it is off. Feeling bitter, I strip in the line to examine my fly, knowing what to expect. Sure enough, the treble hook is partially straightened, bent by the excessive violence of my strike. The momentum of my 16-ft carbon rod moving back at full speed was more than the little size 10 treble could take. It was my own fault that I lost the fish. With a more gentle strike it might well have been landed.

The incident illustrates a number of points. Firstly, salmon do not always take a fly positively. Frequently they will suck it in, and then blow it out again, without ever closing their mouths on it. I have seen this happen many times while watching others fish. Often, when fish are described as rising, or coming 'short', I am sure that this is what has happened. If it occurs when I am fishing, my first inclination is to suspect that there is some fault in the way my fly is presented. It usually suggests that the fly is too large or too slow moving. Correcting the fault will often produce more positive takes.

Secondly, it shows that when you have to strike a fish, you must match the power of the strike to the tackle you are using. The big single irons used for sunk fly fishing, in sizes up to 10/0, by former generations, took a really hefty wallop to get home. It needed all the momentum of a strike with a 16 ft Greenheart rod, probably more than double the weight of today's carbon equipment, to drive the point of the hook in over the barb. With those large hooks, the distance from the point to the barb could be as much as half an inch. However, once home, they rarely fell out. Even today, when using treble hooks of up to size 2 with the sunk fly, I like to apply a firm pull, sustained for at least half a minute, before I can be confident that the fish is properly on. Smaller trebles, such as the size 10 that I normally use with a half-inch tube, do not need anything like so much pressure. In the example I have just described, I should not have clamped the line to the rod butt with my finger. Instead, the line should have been left free, going direct to the reel, which should have been set with the drag just tight enough not to overrun.

It might also have helped if I had used a bit more thought, and made an educated guess about the likely size of the fish. A big fish has far more inertia, so that it is not pulled through the water by a strike, than a small fish. Clearly, a violent strike encountering an immovable object is more likely to damage tackle than one that encounters something more yielding. Often it is the larger than usual salmon, especially if they have been in the river some time and are starting to colour up, that adopt these cat-and-mouse tactics of playing with the fly. Had I been a bit brighter, I would have guessed this, and made a more gentle strike, with the result that I might not have lost a fish that felt as though its weight was well up into the twenties.

Thirdly, the incident shows how essential it is to be able to vary one's tactics, not just in presenting the fly, but in the method used to try to hook the fish as well. My line was nicely slack on the surface of the water, so that if the fish had taken positively there would have been nothing to arouse its suspicions, or to hinder its progress as it turned back to its lie with the fly in its mouth. However, I might have stood there all day, raising the fish every few casts and never hooking it, if I had stuck to the conventional method of waiting for the fish to draw out some line before tightening into it.

Different authorities on salmon fishing advise different ways of hooking the fish. The techniques can really be divided into two camps. Slack liners and strikers. Slack liners include those who fish holding a loop of line to be released when a fish takes, those who keep their rod points high in the air, and wait for the fish to straighten the line curving beneath, those who keep the drag on their reels lightly set and allow the fish to take several yards of line, and lastly those who not only release yards of slack but also wade down the pool till they are level with their fish. Only after the slack (however created) has been taken is the fish tightened into, by raising the rod. The strikers include those who strike firmly, immediately they see or feel a fish, and those who, if they see a rise, allow a brief pause before swinging the rod back. Sadly, there is no single method that works one hundred per cent of the time. This is because of the various ways that salmon can take a fly, the different methods of presentation, and the nature of the place in which it happens. A variety of methods of hooking the salmon will be needed to cope with changing situations, so be prepared to adapt rather than be hampered by adhering dogmatically to a single technique.

The various slack line methods depend on the current pulling the line downstream, thus drawing the hook back into the corner of the fish's mouth. This works well when fishing down and across the stream, provided that it is not flowing too slowly. Problems arise in very slow water, or with fish that take on the dangle directly downstream, or those that eject the fly soon after taking it into their mouths. Slack line methods also tend to be unsuccessful when the angler is drawing in the fly by hand-lining, or using some of the various dragged surface fly or nymph fishing techniques.

Striking may work better when using large hooks, or with fish that take on the dangle, or in slack water: also when hand-lining, or using dragged surface fly or nymphing, and when fish merely play with the fly for a second or two, as opposed to taking it positively. It sometimes works less well when the fly is taken very slowly, as there is a tendency to jerk the hook out of the fish's mouth, something that many former trout anglers find to their dismay, when they take up salmon fishing for the first time.

My own technique varies with circumstances. Typically, I fish with the line going direct to the reel, and when a fish takes, it usually pulls out some line. All I do is to stop the reel and then raise the rod to tighten into the fish. Simplicity in itself.

If I am fishing the floating line, my reel is set at a lighter drag than for the sunk fly, as I will often be using a finer leader, and lighter hooks. The salmon, too, may take a small, slow-moving fly more gently, and slowly than a larger, faster-moving fly. Frequently I do not see the rise, and the first that I know of a fish taking the fly is the line suddenly tightening, and the reel giving a quick buzz. However, if I see a rise, I do nothing until the line moves. When it does, I know that my fly is in the fish's mouth, and that the points of the hook are already lodged against some part of it. I can now put my hand to the reel to hold, stop or slow it, and then start raising the rod.

Small sharp treble hooks tend to catch in the mouth of the fish before they get drawn back into the scissors at the corner of the jaw. Single hooks will tend to slide back into the scissors, which explains the origins of the slack line methods of hooking. Historically, everyone tended to use single hooks, and if one of these was lying flat in the jaws of the fish, a premature strike would simply slide it out from between them. However, if slack line was given, the downstream pull would take the hook back till it lodged securely in the scissors.

With the sunk line, it is rarer for there to be any kind of surface disturbance when a fish takes. Usually there is just a pull, whereupon I stop, or slow, the reel, and raise the rod. Sometimes there is just a growing weight on the line, as if the fly had caught on a rock. This happens when the salmon has only had to rise perhaps a foot in the water to grab the fly, and then sinks slowly back, as the current starts to belly the line downstream. By the time I feel the fish, the hooks have already lodged in part of its mouth, and giving more slack line will not change their position. In any case, if I have felt the fish, it has felt me, and will try to rid itself of the strange object pricking its jaw and somehow pulling its head to one side. So I tend to tighten as soon as I am sure it is a fish. Few anglers would give line to a taking fish while spinning, so why should it be necessary with the sunk fly? When tightening into a fish on the sunk line, it is important to continue to apply pressure until the hook is safely home. It can take a long hard pull to get a large hook to penetrate some of the bony parts of a fish's mouth.

Many anglers find that takes 'on the dangle' are hard to deal with for two reasons. A line hanging straight downstream has no lateral pressure on it, from the current, to draw the hook back into the corner of the fish's mouth. The other reason is that the fish often stops dead in the water immediately after taking the fly. A salmon that takes positively, then turns at once, and swims back to its lie, will be well hooked, usually in the corner of its mouth, if not half-way down its throat, whatever you do, and wherever in the stream it takes your fly. The problem is the fish that stops dead in the water immediately after it has taken the fly. If it happens out in the stream opposite you, this presents no difficulties. The weight of the current on your line will draw the hook back into the fish's mouth. If you are fishing with a floating line, you will probably see the rise, then the far end of your line slowly sinking down into the water, followed by the formation of a downstream belly. Fishing with single hooks and floating line. This has been described by many people as the 'classic rise', leading to salmon well hooked in the corner of the mouth. Fishing with trebles, I find that it can result in fish that are less securely hooked, either in the lower lip or the tongue. If you are fishing with the sunk line, all that you will be aware of is a growing weight on the line, as if your fly had caught on the bottom. When your fly is hanging on the dangle straight downstream, in slack water beside the main current, and a fish takes, then stops where it is, without heading back to its lie, there is no way that releasing more line is going to make any difference, while the fish is stationary. If there is a current, and you move your rod point inshore to try and create the necessary downstream belly to draw the hook back into the scissors, you will be relying on the action of the stream on the few feet of your leader downstream of the fish. This may well exert insufficient leverage to move the hook back into position.

I deal with these takes 'on the dangle' by tightening hard immediately I feel the fish. Holding the reel tightly, I raise the rod firmly. If, as often happens, the fish is pulled towards me, I reel in fast or hand-line to keep the pressure on. If the fish thrashes on the surface, which is another frequent occurrence, I do not give it slack line, but try to apply side-strain from inshore, as the lower angle of the line sometimes encourages it to go back down in the water. It may not always be possible to apply side-strain like this, as a steep bank behind, or trees and bushes can get in the way and there is a risk that the hooks will pop out of the side of the fish's mouth. Once you have started tightening into the fish, you must avoid a slack line until the hooks are safely home. The object is to hook the fish in the front part of the roof of its mouth. Once the hook is home, this is a very secure hold. However, it is bony and tough, and if you do not pull either hard enough, or for long enough, the hook point will not penetrate sufficiently to bury the barb. This will result in the traditional 'lightly-hooked fish that took on the dangle', which escapes after a minute or two, often less.

With fish that take in this way, I am usually not satisfied that the hooks are properly home till I have kept a good hard pull on the fish for at least a minute. If you only hold the fish lightly at first, and wait till it is out in the stream opposite before applying pressure, you will probably pull the hooks out of the side of its mouth. If the fish is straight below you, and you pull with a raised rod, this should draw the hook points up into the roof of its mouth. I lose far fewer fish with this method than I did when I tried to give them slack line when they took on the dangle.

With fish that take when you are stripping in line by hand, you should also not release any slack line, but tighten as soon as you feel it, for it has already felt you, or more accurately, the sharp prick of the hook points, something that it will try to rid itself of at once. This applies equally whether the fish is out opposite you in the pool or down below on the dangle.

With the dragged surface fly, the response to a taking fish will depend on the circumstances. A relatively big fly moving fast across the surface often produces violent takes, and all that you need to do to set the hook is to slow down and stop the reel before raising the rod. Sometimes the take is so savage that this has to be done carefully to avoid a break. With dapping and dibbling, particularly on the short line, you should watch your fly carefully. Violent takes are no problem, the fish will have hooked itself before you can react. However, salmon often take with a slow roll through the surface of the water, just like a lazy brown trout, and here you should watch closely to make sure the fish actually takes the fly into its mouth. Then you should lower your rod point towards the fish so that the line is slack while it turns down in the water. Only when your leader moves, as the fish draws it down into the water should you raise your rod again to tighten into the fish. If you strike too soon, while the fish is still on the surface, you risk plucking your fly out from between its jaws.

With the dry fly, again you must not do anything unless you are sure that your fly is in the fish's mouth. Frequently the fish rises but does not touch the fly, or appears to try to drown it by rolling on top of it, or 'chinning' it with a closed mouth. Only if I see the fish definitely take my fly, and the leader drawing under the surface, do I strike. The concentration required is no more than watching a dry fly when after brown trout, and seeing whether the fish takes the artificial, or a natural fly an inch or two away on the surface of the water.

Fishing the upstream nymph for salmon, it is rare to feel the fish take. I strike as soon as I see any check, or drawing under of the leader or end of the line, just as I would if fishing for trout. Usually, the fish is securely hooked in the top lip or the corner of its mouth.

In general, the colder the water the slower the fish moves, and the longer one can wait before tightening into it. The warmer the water the quicker the fish moves, and the more likely it will be to spit out your fly if you leave it too long before tightening. Running fish often cause problems, taking a quick snap at your fly as they swim upstream. All too often, fishing with a loop of line lightly held between my fingers, it has been drawn out in the classic manner, but when I raised the rod, there was nothing there. I thought there was a need to keep at least some light tension on the fly from the moment after the fish closed its mouth on it, and started to turn away.

This led to my fishing from the reel as I have previously described. When I use the floating line, it generally lies in a curve on the water surface. The combination of this slack line and the fairly lightly set disc drag on the reel, ensures that there is minimal resistance as the fish takes the fly. As it turns down and back towards its lie, it begins to pull line off the reel, and to straighten the curve of the line. Stopping the reel with the palm of my hand, the fish will feel increasing resistance as the curve in the line straightens, and I start to raise the rod to eliminate any remaining slack. The whole process is based on the line not being under tension when the fish takes, and then gradually increasing the resistance as it moves away. I can speed or slow the process at will.

To speed it up, I can set the drag on the reel more tightly, or hold the reel by hand, and raise the rod sooner. To slow the process, I can set the drag more lightly, and allow more time and perhaps several yards of line to be drawn off the reel, before starting to tighten.

Plucks, pulls and lightly hooked salmon are sometimes a serious problem with the sunk fly, either when fish are running up fast through the beat, or in cold water, when they may take very slowly and gently, without seeming to close their mouths properly on the fly. If I am suffering from a series of these missed connections, I can often cure the problem by switching to a smaller treble (with the same tube fly) which penetrates more easily than a large hook. For tubes up to 2$\frac{1}{2}$in long, I normally use a size 4 treble, and with tubes of 3in and over a size 2. Switching to a size 6 means that far less pressure need be applied to draw the hooks home, although some strength and holding power, for large fish and heavy water, may be sacrificed.

However, I am always prepared to experiment with different tactics, and experience helps the process of recognising when to speed up or slow down in response to a series of missed takes. Varying my timing makes me feel better on the bad days, and boosts my morale, because I am at least trying to do something positive about the problem. If I do nothing, the feeling of growing hopelessness as each successive fish gets away can seriously undermine self-confidence. Changing my tactics to try to defeat the problem means that mentally I stay on the attack.

Section 2: Playing the Fish

Seventeenth May 1975. It is a little after 9 p.m., with the evening warm and still after a bright sunny day. I am fishing the Top Gannet at Ballogie on the Dee. Casting a long line, and with much mending to control the flies as they move round, I am standing on the firm shingle in about two and a half feet of fast water at the top of the pool, in order to fish the 'drop-off' into the deep water channel below. In those days, this started up near the top of the pool, about two-thirds of the way across, not too distant from a large and very deep backwater under the far bank. The channel ran straight downstream for over thirty yards before turning sharp right, square across the pool, towards the Ballogie side. A few yards out from this, the south bank, it turned left to flow straight downstream towards the bottom of the pool. The sections of the channel where it ran square across the pool and turned down again, really were very deep. You could stand close to the edge of the shingle and poke a fly rod straight down, tip first, into the black water before you, and not find the bottom. The change from a bright yellow shingle bottom to Stygian darkness took only a yard or so across the drop-off. The deepest parts of the channel were reputed to be over twenty-five feet deep. Salmon lay all over the pool, and at that time it could hold a fantastic stock of fish. The best taking water was along and behind the drop-off. Sadly, the deep channel started to fill with shingle in the mid-1980s, and the drop-off is now only a gentle slope. The pool holds a small fraction of the fish it used to, and is but a shadow of its former glory.

As my flies drift around through the rippled surface of the black water behind the drop-off, there is a sudden violent pull, and several yards of line are ripped from my reel. My heart leaps, I grab the reel, and raise the rod, but there is only light pressure, as the fish has already turned and is heading back upstream. I reel in fast, and tighten into the fish. It has returned to its lie in the deep water below the drop-off.

I bend the rod into the fish, and start to wade towards the bank. About half-way to the shore I stop, for, judging by the slope of my line as it enters the water, if I go much further back it will be running over the edge of the shingle. If that happens, and the fish moves, the line may catch under a stone, which would increase the risks of being broken. So I decide to stay where I am, and to try to get the fish up off the bottom, and moving about in mid-water, before I resume my progress to the bank.

I apply more pressure to the fish, winding in until there is a fair strain on the rod, but nothing happens. The salmon does not move, staying in its place on the bottom of the river. Slowly I increase the tension, winding the rod point down, until it is only two or three feet above the surface of the water, and I am starting to worry about the strength of the leader. Still nothing happens, and I take in a little more line, till most of the rod is pointing straight at the fish, and I know that only another turn or two of the reel will be enough to break the leader. Suddenly, I feel the fish move, at last! But he only takes out a few yards of line, and then stops.

Again I increase the pressure till my nylon leader is near breaking point, and the fish again responds by slowly moving a few yards further away across the pool, staying down at the bottom of the deep water behind the drop-off.

With the fish stationary once more, I increase the strain till it repeats its response by moving a few yards further away. By now I know that I have hooked a 'monster', and I am growing increasingly concerned about the length of line that I have stretched out under water, straight across the pool, and with the full weight of the current bearing on it. If the fish goes much further out, and then makes a dash down or up the stream, I know that I will have major problems with a heavily drowned line.

I do not know how to improve matters. If I head back in for the bank, it will simply increase the amount of line under water. If I try to shorten the line by following the fish out across the pool, I will have to wade upstream against the strong current, and if I manage to make any significant progress against that, I will be left very vulnerable, with a long trip back to the bank, if the fish then decides to make a dash downstream. If I stay where I am, I cannot 'undrown' the line by raising the rod, as I am unable to apply enough pressure on the fish with its tip up in the air. I decide to stay where I am and to hope for the best.

Again I apply maximum pressure on the fish, and again it only moves a few yards further away, holding to the bottom of the river. The process continues, with the fish moving across the pool a little bit at a time in response to the strain of my horizontal rod. Eventually it reaches the deep backwater at the top of the pool on the Kincardine side.

The fish has now been on for some ten minutes, and under the maximum pressure that I can impose for almost all that time, yet not once have I managed to draw the fish towards myself. Its slow movement across the pool has conveyed to me an impression of almost irresistible power.

In the backwater under the far bank, the fish moves slowly upstream against the heavy drag of the current on the drowned line, stretched tight deep under water across the pool. The line ticks slowly off the reel, and then it stops. At last the pressure eases, and I can reel in, slowly, a few yards of line. Then, once more, the strain increases and I know the fish is moving upstream again, as the line is forced slowly from the reel. Although I cannot see it, I know that the fish is circling in the backwater. As he goes upstream, he draws out line, and when he drops back down, I can reel in a little. However, not once do I have the idea that I have gained line by actually pulling the fish towards myself.

The fish continues to circle in the backwater for some time, perhaps another ten minutes, maybe a little longer, and throughout I have been holding him as hard as I dared, with the rod forced down to the horizontal, releasing line only when the leader was in danger of breaking. The lack of progress is worrying me. I keep hoping that the pressure will begin to tell on the fish, and that he will be forced to become more active, to turn and run downstream so that I can lift the drowned line to get into direct contact with him. Above all, I want to see him, to get a sight of this monster. The fish has now been on for more than twenty minutes, and here I am, still stuck in the middle of the river like a fool. Resolving to do something positive, whatever the risks, I start to wade diagonally upstream, to lift and shorten the drowned line.

Struggling hard against the current, I have managed to cover only three or four yards, when, quite suddenly the inevitable happens, and I feel the fly pull out of the fish's mouth. With my fly line and about thirty yards of backing now floating peacefully on the surface of the pool, I turn to wade back down to the bank, feeling sick with disappointment.

So, what lessons can be learned from this excellent example of how not to deal with a very big fish? At the start of the fight I should have waded diagonally downstream till I was safely ashore. I should then have climbed to the top of the bank, more than twenty feet above the river, but with my line entering the water safely downstream of the edge of the drop-off, and fought the fish from up there, rather than from down by the waterside. This would have avoided any danger of my line getting caught up in the shingle, and would also have largely eliminated the problem of the drowned line, so that I would have been able to apply a direct pull to the side of the fish's head.

The current runs more or less squarely downstream over the top edge of the drop-off where it cuts across the pool, but at the bottom, deep under water, the current runs across the pool, along the base of the shingle. This meant that although I was pulling hard from across the river, as far as the fish was concerned, I was only trying to pull it straight downstream, as opposed to pulling it off balance by pressure from the side. If a salmon's head is pulled to one side, so that the fish can no longer point directly upstream, its beautiful streamlined shape is wasted, and it has to use vastly more energy just to hold its place against the current.

Had I applied strong direct pressure from the side, the fish would have been forced into fighting far more actively, so that it tired quicker. With a pull from directly downstream, the fish can adopt a head-down profile, so that it is pressed into the bed of the river by the current, and thus held in place to resist the pull of the line with a minimum of effort.

The other main point concerns the adequacy of the tackle. The rod was a Sharpe's 13-ft split cane, capable of coping happily with fish in the 20 to 30 lb class. However, against a 'monster' of this size, it was neither long nor strong enough to lift the line clear of the water, while applying the pressure required. The fly was a size 6 Thunder and Lightning, and unless a relatively small hook like that lodges firmly into the gristle or bone of the toughest parts of the fish's mouth or throat, it will gradually tear through any softer flesh or skin during the course of a prolonged struggle. The larger the hook size, the wider its gape and the deeper its purchase, and therefore the smaller the chance of its tearing free. Larger hooks also tend to be made from thicker wire than smaller hooks. Again the thicker the wire the slower it will tear through the flesh.

The 12 lb-leader was also too fine for coping with so large a fish. Any weakness such as an abrasion, or even a poorly tied knot, weakens fine nylon proportionally far more than thick nylon. With the strain that I was putting on that fish, my worries about breaking the leader were well founded. I, like many others before me, had no idea as I set out, that I would encounter such a monster. If it has only happened to me once in nearly thirty years of salmon fishing in this country, I could hardly recommend basing every decision about tackle on such a remote possibility. If I ever encounter such a fish again, I can only hope that it will be when I am using my heavy-duty sunk line outfit.

These days, I am quite philosophic about the odds of losing even moderately large fish on the floating line. If I am using my standard $\frac{1}{2}$in tube and size 10 treble, I reckon that anything that takes more than twenty or twenty-five minutes to land is probably going to get off, unless I am very fortunate. It usually takes a little under a minute per pound to play the fish on such tackle, so anything approaching twenty-five lb or over has the odds on its side. However, with the sunk line, I have no such worries, because the hooks are larger and the tackle more robust. I can therefore be harder on the fish, so that it usually takes me only half or two-thirds of the time to land a fish on the sunk line that it would have taken on the floating line.

Many pools have their own particular hazards when it comes to playing fish. Over the years local lore will usually have found a way of dealing with problems such as the piers of bridges, large rocks, old tree stumps, or even the remnants of a line of piling that once protected the bank. A friendly chat with the gillie *before* you start fishing can save a lot of frustration.

Once the hooks are firmly home, the general advice is to head for the bank, so that if the fish takes off downstream, it can be followed. Nowadays, especially in low water, I am in less of a hurry to make for the shore. If the river is very rocky, it is much easier to steer the fish round the boulders on a fairly short line when standing in the water at the edge of the current, than it is to do the same thing with a long line from the bank. Some pools have a wide expanse, perhaps thirty yards, of shallow water only a few inches deep running down their sides. In these conditions, it is often easier to land it quietly in a net, while standing offshore in two or three feet of water, than having to make several attempts to drag the fish protesting across the shallows, with the danger of it unhooking itself on the way. Much depends on the early stages of the fight. If the fish is very active, and charges around all over the river, you should prepare for trouble, and position yourself for a rapid downstream pursuit if it becomes necessary. However, if the fish is quiet, it is usually possible to bring matters to a conclusion without moving more than a few yards from the position where it was hooked.

There will be occasions when you have to walk the fish upstream. Usually this is to avoid hazards immediately below, or obstructions in the area where the fish was hooked. It is best done in the early stages of the fight, before the fish realises what is happening. As soon as you are sure that the hooks are home, lower the rod so that you are applying side-strain from your upstream shoulder. Hold the rod in both hands, pressing the fingers of the lower hand against the rim of the reel to prevent it paying out line. Do not pinch the line against the butt with the fingers of the upper hand. Now, watching carefully where you put your feet, and where the fish is, start to steadily side-step your way upstream. Do not, as some advise, turn round, put the rod over your shoulder and walk upstream. That is a recipe for coming to an abrupt halt, with the fish on one side of a rock, and your line on the other. Do not walk backwards upstream, as you risk a crashing fall and a lost fish, by putting an unguarded foot into a hole in the bank, something that I have done several times. Most of the time it will be easier to walk the fish up while standing on the bank. It may be better to wade upstream if the fish has to be manoeuvred up a route between large boulders to somewhere with greater freedom for action. This is easier with a relatively short line, although difficult to perform in areas with a strong current or hazardous wading.

Walking the fish upstream works because you are applying a strain from diagonally inshore and upstream, thereby 'unbalancing' the fish. It usually responds by trying to point its nose slightly out into the stream away from your pull, and swimming slowly. The compromise between the angle of your pull and the angle of the fish's nose results in its moving more or less straight upstream. Quite often the fish will swim fast enough to overtake the rod, so the walking up process may end with it upstream of you.

Frequently the fish will object, usually by turning out into the current and trying to head downstream again. Try not to let it have any line. Sometimes it is inevitable, but usually it can be prevented by holding the reel firmly, and only allowing the fish to pull the rod down and round. It is much easier to hold a fish if it is not allowed to build up any momentum in the first place, so that a potential run is aborted without getting properly started. Sometimes, despite your best efforts at quietly firm and steady handling, the fish will dash off downstream, and you have little choice but to go after it and start again. When wading, I usually head diagonally upstream to get to the shore, so that by the time I reach the bank, the walking up process is already well under way.

Trying to check or to hold the line by clamping it to the rod butt with your fingers is a bad habit. Once a fish starts to take out line you will get burned or cut fingers if you try to slow it in this way. It is also difficult to release line gradually like this, as it tends to come out in an undesirable sudden jerk. Use the palm of your hand against the rim of the spool, which produces a more even braking effect, and is much easier to control when the fish is under way. A modern disc drag reel is an enormous help in playing a fish. It will release line steadily and evenly as pressure builds up. I usually tighten mine by two or three notches immediately after hooking a fish, and often rely on this alone for holding purposes during the fight.

The angle at which a rod is held makes a considerable difference to the ease with which a fish can draw line off the reel. The greater the angle between the butt of the rod and the direction the fish is pulling, the more the friction between the rod rings and the line, and the less easy it will be to take line off the reel. With a stiffly set drag, a fish may be unable to take out line when the rod is vertical, but able to do so when the rod is lowered. This is of particular importance in the latter stages of a fight, when the fish is being manoeuvred on a short line prior to landing. At this time, the angle between the rod butt and the fish may sometimes approach 180°. If the fish makes a sudden run, the rod point must immediately be lowered, or swung round, towards the direction in which the fish is heading. Failure to do this promptly has resulted in many disasters.

Once the fish is in an area of water in which it can be played relatively safely, it must be kept on the move and not allowed to rest. Stand roughly opposite the fish, and continually try to force it off balance, by pulling its head round towards yourself. This makes it difficult for the fish to hold stationary in the current, and it is likely to run. As soon as it stops, reel in, and do not let the fish hang stationary in the water.

When the fish is upstream of me, I tend to apply side-strain on it from my upstream shoulder. If it is opposite me, I usually keep my rod up, with the butt at an angle of about 45–60° above the horizontal. If it moves down, I switch the rod over to applying side-strain from downstream shoulder. This can help a lot in confusing and therefore controlling the fish.

If the fish is out in midstream and slightly above you, while you apply side-strain from the upstream shoulder, and it makes a sudden bolt downstream, swing your rod over immediately, keeping the pressure on the whole time, so that you are now applying side-strain from your downstream shoulder. This will frequently pull the fish off course, so that it arcs round towards you, temporarily bewildered by the change of direction. It can end up less than twenty yards away from you, whereas, if you had kept the rod in the same position, or only moved it round when the fish was well below, you might not have halted its run till it was more than fifty yards downstream.

If a big fish drops down a heavy stream broadside on, the force of the current may mean you cannot hold it. You must go downstream with it, pulling hard from opposite it, at right angles to the current. Only when the fish has been turned, so that it is again aligned up and down the stream, will you be able to recover line.

If a salmon does make a positive and sustained rush downstream, get after it as quickly as possible. It is far better to do this than to have the fish rampaging around 150 yards below you, and unable to prevent its going round a rock, or some other disaster. A salmon finds it much easier to swim against a pull from directly behind, than against one at right angles to its line of progress. So keep the strain on the fish when you set off after it, and try to draw level as soon as possible. Following the fish along a steep bank, there are likely to be two paths, one along the bottom, which is usually strewn with pitfalls in the shape of boulders and pot-holes, and one along the top, which often takes quite an effort to climb up to, but is generally smoother when you get there. I have slipped or fallen so many times when pursuing fish, especially late in the evening, that I normally try to take the high road these days. When you draw level with the fish, do not stop immediately, but keep going a little longer, increasing the pressure on the fish with your rod, if you can, till you are in front (i.e. downstream) of it. A salmon travelling downstream at speed has less control of his direction, and now you should easily be able to pull him round, bringing him to a stop, probably on your side of the current, and several yards upstream.

Salmon will usually try to swim away from a pull, so applying a gentle strain from below will often persuade a fish to swim upstream, and sometimes to tow you back up to where you started from, even after a hectic dash down the bank.

If there is an impassable obstruction below you, beyond which a fish cannot be followed, the best tactic is never to allow it to go down in the first place. It is much easier to prevent a fish from running than it is to stop it once it has started. Schoolboy physics states that momentum equals mass times velocity, so if a fish is held stationary in the water, you will only have to counter the thrust of its tail and the effect of the current. Once it is under way, its momentum may render it impossible to stop. If you hold it so hard that it cannot run but merely thrashes in the water, quite substantial fish can be held like this in emergency, provided they are on a short line. On a longer line, the fish has a much bigger arc through which it can swim, and so pick up speed, and is therefore much more difficult to hold. The biggest problems with holding a substantial fish (anything much above 20 lb) really hard on a short line come when the fish makes an abrupt change of direction. If your response is not quick enough, you can so easily be broken. However, I would rather lose a fish through holding it too hard than allow it to go down a waterfall or rapid.

If the fish does get below where you cannot follow it, you have two basic courses of action after it has stopped. The first is to steadily reel, and walk it back up the river. This can be very difficult with a big fish at the end of a long line in a heavy current. The second is to allow another twenty yards or so of line to peel off your reel, bellying downstream in the current. This will pull on the salmon from below, encouraging it to swim upstream. As a tactic it is fraught with danger. At the end of more than 100 yards of line it is very difficult to see what is happening, and you have no control over the movements of the fish. Your line is likely to be drowned, and could easily become snagged around a rock. If the fish is tired, it may no longer be able to swim upstream, towing the line up against the drag of the current, in which case it will probably start dropping downstream again . . .

Some anglers recommend the tactic of releasing line to stop and turn a fish heading downstream. This can only work if the fish is travelling downstream slower than the current, otherwise there is no way that the line can form a belly below it.

Being too gentle on the fish may lead to sulking. When this happens, the salmon adopts a nose down attitude in the water, with its tail high, and it body slanting down and slightly across the current. At this angle, the pressure of the current pushes the fish down and away from the angler, who is normally upstream of the fish at an angle of about 45°. Pressed into its adopted position by the current, it can sustain this with very little effort for a long time. Typically, the angler, standing with his rod bent into an immobile fish, grows increasingly worried about the hook hold with each minute that passes. He becomes less and less inclined to take the necessary corrective action while growing ever more desperate. Meanwhile the fish is having a nice rest. I once watched someone take just under an hour and a quarter to land a 14 lb salmon that did this. Had he taken the appropriate steps, it would have lasted an hour less. The solution is to move down the bank till you are opposite, or slightly below the fish. Then pull firmly, and reel in as you shift it from its position. Its head will be drawn round towards you, and the current will also be pushing it in your direction rather than making it otter away. To prevent your drawing it into the side, the fish will have to do some work, and swim actively up and away into the current.

After the hooks are home, if a fish lashes the surface shaking its head, it is often a sign that it is being played too hard, and is being held too tightly. A slight easing of the pressure, allowing the fish to make a run usually cures the problem. If you are standing in the boulder-strewn torrent immediately above the lip of a waterfall, or in some other emergency situation, it is worth noting that a fish that lashes the surface in this way is not in control of its movements. Even a substantial fish can sometimes be dragged in, while it is flailing on the surface. It is definitely not a tactic recommended for normal use, because of the high risk of the hook tearing free, but in desperate circumstances I have certainly used it to gain a few invaluable yards of line, and once or twice even to draw a fish into the net.

The series of unpleasant jerks from deep in the water can be very worrying. Sometimes they are caused by the fish shaking its head violently with its mouth wide open. Sometimes they are caused by the fish rubbing its mouth against a rock, or even turning on its side to push its mouth against the bottom of the river. If there is an outside hook of the treble projecting from the fish's mouth, and the

Concealment

Top: Standing within a yard of the bank less than knee deep keeps the angler below the skyline when there is a flat bank behind. The author fishes the sunk fly at Anne's Seat on the Don.

Bottom: Concealment is less important on big rivers and where high banks or a steep slope behind provides a solid background to make the angler less obvious to the fish. The author, handlining at Rurholm, River Vosso.

Playing the fish

A hooked salmon heading downriver at Syre on the Naver. The author swings his rod over to apply sidestrain from his downstream shoulder (B), which confuses the fish, so that it stops its downstream rush, and turns, swirling the surface (C). The author then leads the fish back upstream, around and down into the waiting net (D), with the rod point kept high to avoid snagging the dropper in the net. Note the dropper, visible just above the author's shoulder (F).

Presentation

Top: Nymph style presentation. A small fly allowed to sink into the backwater behind the point here at Anne's Seat on the Don, and then drawn up as it crosses the deep water channel, will often be taken by a salmon resident in this superficially unattractive and very slow water.

Bottom left: Controlling the line with an upstream mend to drop the flies downstream more slowly than the current.

Bottom right: Sink and draw, nymph style. The author has just shaken loose line out through the rod rings to allow the flies to sink again.

Landing the fish

Top: When netting a fish, always crouch down to maintain the lowest of profiles. Here, the salmon has seen the upright gillie and makes a panic-stricken dash out into the stream. Despite using sidestrain, the author is unable to hold it. Several minutes must pass before this 15½lb salmon is safely in the net.

Bottom: Large nets can be manipulated with ease by the single handed angler. The author nets a small salmon from the Dart in Devon.

point catches on a rock, the fish can unhook itself in a fraction of a second. Even worse, the jerks are sometimes accompanied by a horrible scrape and twang as the leader slides across a rock.

The jerks, or jags, may be caused by the fish bashing the leader with its tail. Some writers have dismissed this as accidental, or unintentional on the part of the fish. It is not. The fish does it deliberately. I remember playing a thirteen-pounder in the Lower Inchbare. It was a bright afternoon, and, with the sun behind me, I could see my leader clearly in the water. The fish played in the deepish water close into the bank below the big rock near the bottom of the pool. It would not run, but merely bored away under the rod tip, head down. From my vantage point above the fish I could see it clearly, manoeuvring itself and slapping at the leader with its tail. Every time I changed the angle of the line by shifting the rod, or moving a few yards along the bank, the fish would change its orientation so that it could again hit the leader with its tail. It was very educational, but I landed the fish.

All forms of head shaking, or jagging, from deep in the river are best dealt with by changing the angle of strain on the fish. Move smartly up or down the bank, and apply side-strain from the opposite shoulder, pulling firmly, so that the fish has to give up what it is doing, and swim actively to hold its place. Jagging and head shaking are very often signs that the fish is not being played firmly enough.

With a salmon that jumps clear of the water, I usually lower the rod towards it if it jumps away from me. Then, if the fish turns a somersault, and catches the line round its body or tail as it turns over in the air, the hook will not be torn from its mouth. If the fish jumps either up or downstream the line should be coming from the side of its mouth and so will usually avoid being caught by the body of the fish as it turns over, and lowering the rod towards it becomes less necessary unless the line is drowned. If a fish jumps a lot during the fight, it may suggest that it is being played too hard, and a slight easing of the pressure will make it less violent. Fresh hen fish seem to jump more frequently than cock fish.

The way that fish play is significantly influenced by the water temperature. In cold water, runs tend to be shorter and the fight more dour, and less spectacular. The fish tend not to jump very often, although they may roll on the surface as they tire. As the water warms up through the 40sF, runs become faster and longer, with the fish jumping more frequently. As a rule I do not expect many really wild fish till the water temperature has reached towards the middle 50sF. Then I have had some spectacular contests, with fish even as small as 8 or 10 lb charging seventy yards across the river at speed, not once, but sometimes several times in the course of a fight.

Whatever the fish, and wherever you play it, you must not let it rest, because this can prolong the fight far longer than the period it was allowed to rest. The longer the fish is on the hook, the more chance it has of getting off.

Do not allow yourself to be intimidated by hooking a big fish. I have seen people play them far more delicately than they would with a fish a third of the size. Be very firm. If you not, the fish is likely to be fresher after an hour's play than you are. By that time, unless the hook hold is exceptionally good, it will be down to the merest sliver of flesh. Try to keep it on a fairly short line, as this will help you manoeuvre it round rocks etc. It also makes it easier to turn the fish if it starts dropping down the current broadside on, when it is tired towards the end of the fight. If you have only a light hook-hold on a big fish it is going to get off however hard or soft you play it. If you have a good hook-hold, being firm with the fish will increase your control over it, and lessen the chances of its breaking the leader over a rock (or any other such dire catastrophe) and therefore increase your chances of landing it. Much better to lose a big fish after ten minutes firm and positive play, trying to assert your mastery, than to lose it after an hour and ten minutes helpless dithering.

If you hook a fish when using two flies on the floating line, try to find out as soon as possible whether it is on the dropper or on the tail fly. This is very important when trying to manoeuvre the fish in shallow rocky water, where a trailing tail fly can easily get caught up. Where there is a chance of this happening you must keep the fish moving to prevent the fly sinking, and try to confine the play to deeper water, to avoid rocks or vegetation on which the fly might snag. Also keep your net out of the way, as the trailing fly could so easily catch in the mesh if you try to net the fish when it swims past just out of range.

Occasionally I encounter a fish that simply will not run but hangs doggedly beneath the rod tip, and insists on swimming under the bank or among the boulders close into the shore. If the water under the bank is deep, such a fish can take a disproportionately long time to play, as pressure can only be applied from directly above it, which is much less effective than from the side. If you have a gillie who can get below you with the net, it should be landed without too much trouble. If you are by yourself, you can easily waste a lot of time. If the water is not too deep, I try to hold the fish upstream of me with the rod, while I wade in below it with the net.

One last point, in the latter stages of a fight, do not try to apply extra leverage by grasping the rod up near its middle section. I have seen several people who do this regularly. It is a very dangerous tactic. You are effectively bending the rod over a fulcrum, something for which it was definitely not designed.

Consistently successful playing of salmon is a product of experience, so that, instinctively, one is neither too hard, nor too soft, on the fish. It is helped by planning in advance how and where you wish to play and land the fish. Having the right tackle to cope with the fish, and the river, is also important. Being prepared to admit, and to learn from one's errors, means that it is less likely that such 'bad luck' will lose more salmon in the future.

Section 3: Landing the Fish

As the fight progresses, the fish tires, its movements become slower, it occasionally rolls on or under the surface, and even turns on its side as it loses control for brief periods. The angler will now be preparing himself to land the fish, which he can do in a number of ways. These include beaching or hand-tailing, using a net, gaff, or mechanical tailer.

Beaching and hand-tailing are inextricably linked. The technique is simplicity in itself. When the fish is so played out that the angler is in complete control, and can slide it helplessly through the water, he merely walks backward, towing the fish downstream into a shelving beach. The fish's nose slides up out of the water, and it gives a last couple of flaps with its tail, which combine with the steady pressure of the angler's rod to help draw most of the fish's body ashore. It lies quiet. Reeling in, the angler walks down to the fish, stoops, and grasps it firmly by the wrist of its tail. He then immediately pushes the fish up the beach till it is completely clear of the water, before lifting it off the ground to carry it up the bank.

I prefer a shelving beach to a wide expanse of shallow water when it comes to drawing the fish ashore. If it has to be towed in across yards of stony water only a few inches deep, the fish will sometimes wake up and start flailing about in a flurry of spray, and the hook can easily get knocked out of its mouth in the confusion. The definition of beach is elastic, and encompasses any surface that slopes into the water and is not too steep to drag a fish up, or across. Mud, sand, gravel, grass, shingle, rock: any will serve. A gap a few inches wide separating a couple of rocks is enough if the fish can be slid out of the water between them.

If there is a steep bank behind, it may not always be possible to walk backwards to tow your fish into the desired spot. You will have to swing it in with your rod, in which case it will be easier if you move the fish round upstream of yourself and then bring it down into the shore with the current behind it.

When you grasp it by the tail, be sure to push the fish up the beach so that it is fully ashore before you try to pick it up. Then, if it slips from your grasp, it will not fall straight back into the river. I remember beaching a fish a few ounces under twenty pounds in the Top Gannet. I walked down and picked it up by the tail to carry it up the bank. As I lifted the fish, my hand and fingers were suddenly seized by acute cramp, and the fish slipped from my grasp, to fall back into the water with a splash. Thinking itself to be free, it promptly bolted out into the river. Fortunately it was well hooked, and I immediately lowered the rod to my right, to apply side-strain from my downstream shoulder. This turned the fish, and it came round, at speed, in an elegant semi-circle, like a water skier on the end of a tow rope, and shot up the beach. This time there was no mistake, and I walked down to the fish, gripped the wrist of its tail firmly with my other hand, pushed it completely out onto the shingle, and then carried it safely up the bank.

It is possible to tail a fish without beaching it first. This is when you have a steep bank, with no visible areas on which you can get the fish's nose ashore, or when thick growth of reeds, rushes, or even clumps of alder and willow render it impossible to get the fish beached in safety. If I am tailing a fish in this way while wading, I like to stand in calm water about two and a half feet deep. If ashore, I will probably have to sit, kneel or even lie on the bank to get down to the fish.

The fish has to be utterly played out, so that it is sliding helplessly through the water on its side, before an attempt to tail it can be made. It is pointless to make futile grabs at the fish as it swims past just out of range. When it is exhausted and lying inert in the water, use your stronger hand to grasp it firmly by the wrist of the tail, and carry it ashore. I do not think it makes any difference which way round your hand is, i.e. thumb closest to the head or to the tail of the fish. Wearing a glove, or wrapping a handkerchief around your hand to improve your grip is not necessary either. Tailing a fish like this is not really suitable for large salmon. Firstly they take so long to play to complete exhaustion, and secondly, even the strongest man will find it difficult to keep his grip sufficiently tight to carry any fish much over 25 lb by the tail with one hand for more than a very short distance.

Being brought up on the Aberdeenshire Don, I soon came to the conclusion that a large landing net was the most practical method of bringing the fish ashore. This is because many of our pools either have steep banks, or in summer the shores are completely overgrown with grass and reeds.

I have read many times that landing nets for salmon are too cumbersome, awkward, and unwieldy for use by the angler fishing alone. I disagree. I used one as a schoolboy, and I know various lady anglers who use them with great efficiency. It does not take brute strength, or the use of both hands, to wield a landing net effectively.

It might help to consider some of the requirements of a good net, before I describe how to use one.

1 It must be large enough to cope with fish in the 25–30 lb class. This implies that if it is circular, the diameter must be at least 2 and preferably $2^1/_2$ ft.
2 The mesh must be deep enough (at least 3 ft) to prevent a salmon wriggling out, if the net has to be dragged vertically up a steep bank.
3 The mesh must be easily replaceable if it becomes rotten or torn through use, although it should be stout enough not to be damaged easily in the first place.
4 Both the handle and the frame of the net must be constructed of a strong, lightweight, non-corroding material.
5 The frame of the net must not be of a folding or collapsible design. If it is, it will inevitably become snarled up during your hour of need. A rigid frame is also a help in acting as a scoop to slide the salmon into the net.

6 If the frame of the net is supposed to slide down the handle in order to extend it for use, the operation must be easily possible, using one hand and a foot, to get it into position. If it cannot be done like this, the net must be carried slung across your shoulders extended ready for use.

7 When the frame is slid into position at the end of the handle, it must lock positively into place. If it does not, and you push the net against the bottom of the river, or against a rock, while trying to land a fish, the frame will simply slide back up the shaft. This will probably leave the salmon flapping about, with its head just over the rim, but not quite close enough for you to get its body inside, while an outside hook of the treble projecting from its mouth can catch in the netting.

8 To be absolutely perfect, the frame and handle of the net should be finished in a dark, non-reflective colour so as not to alarm the fish more than necessary during the latter stages of the fight.

9 The net does not require a fancy sling to be carried across your shoulders. I use two pieces of stout nylon cord. The longer one is attached to the handle. One end of the shorter piece is attached to the base of the frame, and the other end to a large stainless steel split ring, of the kind that can be bought for a few pence in any hardware shop. A simple slip knot, to join the end of the long piece to the ring, makes a sling that is robust, cheap, easy to use, and infinitely adjustable.

You will want to unship your net at some point during the latter stages of the fight so that you are ready when the opportunity comes. If you use a sling of the type I have described, when you undo the slip knot, the net should slide round conveniently under your arm. If you hold the rod in your left hand, the shaft of the net can be trapped under your right armpit and supported on your right forearm. With the net held in this way, you can continue to reel in, or move along the bank at will.

You should have already selected the place where you intend to net the fish. Ideally, this should be an area of calm water about 2–3 ft deep, several yards back from the edge of the main current, and relatively free of obstructions. It is better to net your fish while standing in the river, because this greatly extends your reach beyond what you can achieve from the bank. If, in your selected area, there happens to be a nice large boulder, tuck yourself in place a few feet below it. You will use it to hide yourself, and your net, from the salmon. If there is no rock, maintain a low profile by crouching down, or kneeling, and avoid sudden movements as far as possible. Do not, ever, make slashes at the fish with net as it comes past, just out of range. If the fish is alarmed by you or the net, it will dash off out into the stream, which may add several minutes to the fight. So keep calm, and remember that concealment works in your favour. A net is an ambush for the fish, and a lot of its value will be lost without the element of surprise.

When you are in position, make sure the bag of the net is wet, by dipping it briefly in the river. If you omit this, it may float, and balloon up through the frame. If this happens, simply turn the net over so that the bag of the mesh is once more hanging freely below the frame. Always check that the mesh is free and not twisted or snarled up in any way. It is not necessary to put a stone in the bottom of the net to make it sink. This will simply make it less manoeuvrable. Keep the net supported by your arm until you need it. Do not rest the rim of the net against the bed of the river while you reel in or manoeuvre the fish, because it will inevitably fall in, and may even be swept away by the current.

When the fish is sufficiently tired, and on a short line, use your rod to swim it round upstream of yourself. (Netting a fish downstream of yourself tends to be tricky, and usually results in failure.) With the fish several yards upstream, turn it, and lead it straight downstream. Now grip the handle of the net about 18in from the end. Those 18in spare should rest against the underside of your forearm, locking the net into a firm grip; a position in which it is easily manipulated. Slip the net into the water at a shallow angle, and, with your rod, continue to bring the fish downstream till its head and then its dorsal fin have passed safely over the rim. Only then should you begin to raise the net. With the fish in the bag of the net, and the rim a foot or more clear of the surface, strip 2 or 3 yards of line from your reel, so there is no pressure on your rod tip. Then if your right hand is holding the net handle, slide it along the shaft until it reaches the join with the frame. If it is a big fish, your left hand, which is holding the rod, can also be used to support the far side of the rim. Do not try to lift the fish at arms length, or with the handle of the net unsupported. With your rod tip carefully pointed out of harm's way you can walk ashore with your fish.

If, when leading the fish down to the net, you are drawing it past a boulder that is helping to conceal your presence, take the fish down outside rather than inshore of the boulder. Do not hold your net too deep in the water. A strong stream will press it down, and so make it far more difficult for you to manipulate. If the fish is up near the surface, you only have to slide your net into the water at a shallow angle, which allows it to be manoeuvred accurately in even the fastest of currents.

The fish will need to be fairly well played out for you to move it around comfortably near the surface of the water. However, providing you take care not to alarm the fish by showing yourself or your net to it, you will often be able to land it a minute or two sooner with a net than by beaching it. But take care. If the fish starts to thrash seriously, or makes a dive for deep water while you are leading it towards the net, get your net out of the way immediately. If an outside hook of the treble, or a trailing dropper or tail fly snags in the netting it is goodbye to the fish. So, be very cautious in your handling of fish that are not fully tired out. I have occasionally managed to trick a salmon into the net within a minute or two of hooking it, but I do not recommend this as a tactic for general use!

Lastly, if netting the fish from the bank, make sure the mesh does not get caught up in any underwater vegetation, tree roots or branches. I remember an incompetent gillie who lost a fish for me by doing just that, when I was fishing the Boat Pool at Carlogie one year. The water was quite high, and the fish was hooked some way down the pool, where a number of alder bushes on the bank had been cut back. The fish was only about 10 lb, well hooked in the scissors, and I soon had control. I brought it in to the side where the gillie was waiting. With the fish over the net, he tried to lift it, but could not, because the mesh was tangled in the alder roots. The fish, half in and half out of the net, began to struggle. An outside hook of the treble caught in the netting and the fish twisted free, leaving the maxillary bone from the side of its mouth still impaled on the hook, as my only souvenir of a salmon that ought not to have been lost.

When I was a boy, gaffing was the standard method for landing salmon. Fortunately, its use has declined substantially since then, because I consider it a barbarous practice, and I would happily support a ban on its use in this country. Gaffing a fifty-pounder in a Norwegian torrent can be justified as the most practical method of landing the fish, but such an event is so rare in this country that I do not think that carrying a gaff is really acceptable these days. However, increasing numbers of anglers now holiday abroad, and may find themselves fishing where gaffing is the norm.

If you have not used one before, get some practice in, to make sure you get it right first time. Tie a log, about $2^1/_2$ ft long and 4 in thick to the end of your line. (A bit of an old fence post will do nicely.) Practise gaffing that, manoeuvring the log around in the stream with your rod and line. Twenty minutes work should ensure there are no mistakes when you have to do it for real. The same technique can be used to help familiarize yourself with any other mechanical means (i.e. a net, or a tailer) of landing your fish.

For gaffing your own fish, it should be lying broadside on to you, aligned parallel with the bank, head pointing upstream. If you are on the right bank, it is best to hold the rod in your left (upstream) hand, and the gaff in your right. If you are on the left bank, hold the rod in your right hand, and the gaff in your left. This will avoid the risk of gaffing across the leader. If you are gaffing someone else's fish, stand several yards below, and have them bring the fish upstream to you, parallel with the bank. Wait till its head is upstream of the gaff, so the stroke can be made from behind the leader as opposed to over the top of it. If you make the stroke over the leader, and miss, the leader will be caught up in the head of the gaff, which will probably result in disaster.

The fish should be near the surface. Do not try to gaff a salmon a couple of feet down in the water. Point downwards, the head of the gaff should be brought down into the water, and then drawn firmly, and slightly upwards, into the fish, in a deliberate stroke, rather than a hasty slash. Ideally the point of the gaff should enter low down at the back of the fish's head, to avoid marring the flesh. Gaffing the salmon in the mid-part of its body means a bigger target, but it is very unsightly. Never try to gaff a fish near the tail. With the point of the gaff firmly home, the fish is then drawn ashore, and lifted up the bank. Gaffing a fish is really two separate operations, first the stroke, then drawing it ashore; it is not a single hooking slash of a movement. Lastly, do make sure your grip on the gaff is firm enough to hold the fish when it kicks.

Many anglers use a mechanical tailer. This is a wire snare, usually attached to a length of springy metal at the end of a fairly short handle. While aesthetically more pleasing than the gaff, its operation is more complex than either the landing net, or beaching and tailing the fish by hand.

With the salmon well played out, the angler brings it round near the surface of the water, usually with its head upstream and only a couple of feet away. He then passes the snare of the tailer over the tail of the fish and along its body until it is roughly half-way between the tail and the dorsal fin. He then lifts smartly, which springs the tailer, partially tightening the noose of the snare, which slides into place around the wrist of the fish's tail. The angler continues to lift and pull back so that the snare tightens fully and the fish is drawn ashore and up the bank.

It is when things go wrong that the tailer comes into its own as a unique method of creating disasters. The first, and least serious of these is when the angler bungles the attempt and springs the snare of the tailer too soon. This can happen for a number of reasons, such as the tailer coming in contact with a rock, the angler starting to lift before the snare is properly in place, or the fish gives a flap with its tail as the angler tries to pass the snare over it. The outcome is the same in all cases. The tailer has been sprung, and must be reset with one hand. This is not particularly difficult if the handle of the tailer is tucked under one arm, or gripped firmly between the legs. However, with his other hand, the angler is still trying to play and control the salmon, and most of us find it difficult to do two things at once. A moment's inattention results in the rod point being lowered, the fish gives a little jerk on a direct line, and the already weakened hook-hold gives way. There is a higher than normal probability of the fish escaping while an attempt to reset the tailer is being made.

The really spectacular disasters occur when the snare of the tailer is sprung when it is too far up the body of the fish, i.e. it is in front of the dorsal fin, not behind it. The noose then tends to slide down over the head and nose of the fish, and the angler finds that he has succeeded in snaring his own line, but the fish is still swimming around in the river. This is when the fun begins, and there is scope for an impressive variety of disasters.

The fish, stirred by the assault, will have found fresh energy, and will be making a last desperate getaway attempt. It will be pulling the line and the rod tip down into the tight snare of the tailer. To avoid a break, the angler can try a number of courses of action. He can release the tailer, which will slide down the line till the snare comes to rest on the fish's nose, causing it to panic further. He will then have to try to bring the fish and the tailer back inshore with his rod, hoping the tailer does not snag in the bottom or unhook the fish before he can attempt to hand-tail or beach it. He can hold on to the tailer, put his rod down quickly, and attempt to hand-line the fish in; or, having put the rod down, he can reset the tailer, take it over the rod tip and back down the entire length of the rod, so that both are free once more. Assuming the fish is still hooked, the angler can then have another go at bringing it into the side and tailing it.

I did once watch someone tail a fish the wrong way round. This happened one day when I was fishing the Sands at Ballogie. An angler, who I had not seen before, or since, was fishing from the Kincardine side with a spinner. He hooked a salmon, and played it, till it was lying exhausted in the water alongside the bank. He then took his tailer, placed the loop over the butt of his rod, which he then positioned on the bank behind him, while he ran the loop up the length of the rod, and over the tip. Holding his rod by the butt once more, he then ran the loop of the tailer down the line and over the head and body of the fish (which was still lying quietly beside the bank) before lifting to draw the snare tight around its tail, and carry it up to the hut. To say that I watched his novel approach in a state of mild astonishment is probably an understatement!

My preferred methods for landing salmon are either with a landing net, or beaching and hand-tailing. Success usually depends on playing the fish quietly but firmly, and on keeping out of its sight. Lastly, it is generally wise not to try to land a fish before it is ready, unless you have to, or you are exceptionally competent.

Part 6 — The Anatomy of a Day on The Dee

To illustrate how I combine preparation, presentation, and persistence in practice, I will describe the course of a typical day's fishing. Avoiding both blanks and bonanzas, I open my fishing diary at random to choose a suitable day. It is 11 May 1989.

I arrive at the main hut by the Potarch Bridge, a little before half past eight on a chilly morning. The sky is overcast, with a cold wind from the east. It smells raw, and I am sure that it will not be long before there is rain, heavy rain. When it comes from the east, it usually lasts for a good twenty-four hours in Aberdeenshire. The Dee is low, down at 1ft 1in on the gauge under the bridge, and, at 48°F, substantially warmer than the air at 39°F.

Tom, the gillie, appears as I am pulling on my waders, and we chat as he busies himself about the hut, opening the shutters on the windows, and tidying away odds and ends. I will be fishing below the bridge today, and neither of us is particularly optimistic, as the river is way below its best height for this half of the beat. Having dressed to cope with the coming cold and wet, I am busy replacing the leader on the floating line, when the other members of the party begin to appear, and we exchange our usual friendly insults by way of greeting, to start the day.

I decide to try the Bridge with the floating line initially. It is a deep pool which usually has a glassy surface, but is now nicely rippled by the east wind. I march out across the bare shingle, to start with a short line at the top of the pool, using the central pier of the bridge to conceal myself from any fish lying close in. The top of the pool is narrow, but it broadens out lower down. Near the tail, the current divides into two main streams, one that flows down parallel to the far bank, and one that flows diagonally into our side of the river. To avoid this nearside stream dragging my flies (two half-inch Hairy Mary tubes) too fast through the water, I cast down and across at an angle of about 45°, fairly vigorously to turn the flies over properly into the east wind. I then put in a big upstream mend, and keep the rod point high to hold the line clear of the water on the nearside. This, with the help of the upstream wind, allows me to control the speed at which my flies drop down and across the current on the far side of the pool. When they reach the stream on the nearside, I control the speed at which they fish across it by moving my rod. I fish right the way down the pool without a touch, and without seeing any sign of a salmon, not even the quick splash of a running fish. The two draws, where the stream flows out of the tail of the pool, can often produce a fish when they are running, but not today.

Gathering my rods, I walk down the bank to fish the Burn of Angels. This used to be a good holding pool, with four groynes on our side to help channel the water. However, many years ago these fell into disrepair, and were washed out by the river. Nowadays, only scattered piles of rocks under the water tell of their former existence. It is rare now for the pool to hold any significant stock of fish, and the odd one or two that pause while they run up is all that I can expect. With the river this low, only the bottom third of the pool is deep enough to offer a temporary resting place to a salmon. I wade down, about a rod's length out from the bank, to help hold my fly where the fish usually lie, about twenty-five yards out into the stream. The water looks attractive, and is nicely rippled, but again there is no sign of a fish. Finishing the tail of the pool carefully with the floating line, I decide that the next pool down, the Floating Bank, is too low to hold fish, and I make up my mind to try the Burn of Angels again, but with the sunk line. To confirm my suspicions, I re-take the temperature of the water. It is 47°F, down 1° from when I took it first thing in the morning.

While I have been fishing, the heavy grey clouds of the overcast sky have been getting steadily lower, and now the first small patches of mist appear on the slopes of the hills. 'It won't be long now', I think, as I wade in to fish the pool with a 2-in brass tube on a sink tip line. Sure enough, less than ten minutes later, I feel the first cold brush of thin grey drizzle on my face. I put up the hood on my rain top, check my cuffs are tight, and carry on. Although I am sure my fly is fishing deep enough, and at the right speed, there is still no response, and I decide to return to the Bridge Pool.

Here I use the full sinker at the top of the pool, with a 1½in brass tube, before switching to the sink tip about a third of the way down, where the current slows as the pool broadens. However, there is again no sign of any salmon throughout my steady progress down the entire length of the pool. The drizzle thickens into a heavy shower of cold rain, before easing again after quarter of an hour.

Having gathered my tackle together, I drive round to the Inchbares. There is a small hut here, and in it I deposit my bag and picnic lunch, before starting to fish the upper part of the pool. This is a shallow, rocky run, with one groyne at the top, and another, now fallen into disrepair, at the bottom, separating it from the Lower Inchbare. Most of it is only about three or four feet deep at this height.

I elect to use the same sink tip line and heavy brass tube, because I will need its weight to get down in the water, while being able to lift the floating body of the line clear of the rocks. I start by standing well back from the end of the groyne at the top of the pool, and fishing with a short line, as the salmon often lie close in. I lengthen line gradually, and move out to the end of the groyne, taking care not to get snagged on the rocks jutting out of the water on my side of the stream. Casting a long line square across the pool, I put in an upstream mend as soon as it hits the water, shooting a bit of spare line as I do so. This provides enough slack to let my fly sink to its proper depth in the water opposite me. The upstream mend, helped by the east wind and my high rod point, prevents the current from dragging my fly too swiftly across the fast water.

As I start to wade the edge of the slack water behind the groyne, the drizzle again turns to rain, and I note that the clouds have dropped lower on the hills. The wind seems to be picking up, and I know that a very wet afternoon is in prospect.

Lower down the pool, where the stream is gentler, I do not need to put in an upstream mend to slow my fly, and indeed I start hand-lining to keep it moving nicely, when it has come round to an angle about 20° out from the bank. I fish the water very thoroughly around, and behind, the line of rocks that separates the Upper and Lower Inchbares, as running fish often choose to stop here for a while. By the time I reach the remains of the groyne separating the two halves of the pool, I have still not seen any sign of a fish, nor has there been any response to my fly.

I toy with the idea of going back down using the floating line, but decide against it, despite the rain easing off again. Not having seen a salmon all morning, lunch seems the more attractive prospect, and I retire to the hut for my sandwiches and a can of beer. Sitting inside the door, I can keep an eye on the pool in case a fish should show, while still being sheltered from the wind and rain, which I know will return ere long.

Before the twenty minutes that it takes me to consume my lunch have passed, the rain is rattling on the tin roof of the hut, and dark cat's paws of wind are driving occasional heavier bursts up river. Re-taking the water temperature, I find it has dropped a further degree to 46°F, and I decide to stick to the sunk line. I replace the 2in brass tube on the sink tip with a 1½in one of the same pattern. The lower half of the pool is rather slower and deeper than the top half, but has large rocks on which the unwary can get caught up.

I resume fishing, casting not too long a line, allowing the fly to sink, swing across some of the pool, and then start gently hand-lining before it reaches the slower water which extends some fifteen or more yards out from the bank. Despite the low water and gentle current, any fish are most likely to be around the edge of this slacker water. I fish right the way down the length of the pool, carefully searching the water, without any response. It is raining steadily now, and the upstream wind has strengthened enough to make casting a long line difficult. Again I think about trying the floating line, but decide against it. I still have not seen a fish, and unbidden, the idea is growing in my mind that I ought to be fishing the lower pools on the beat. This is a better sign, and long ago I learned to pay attention to hunches like that.

So, loading everything into the car again, I drive round to the car park above the Kelpie and the Bulwarks. A member of the 'opposition' on the Sluie bank is already fishing the Kelpie, so I head for the Bulwarks.

In the Middle Bulwark, I start by wading out above, and nearly as far as the pointed rock in the stream at the top of the pool. Even though I am approaching two-thirds of the way across the river, the water is not as deep as my knees. At this height, the salmon tend to lie in the fast deep water between the bulwark on the far bank, and the rock, and for about ten yards in this same stream, below the bulwark.

With a 2in brass tube again on the sink tip, I cast into the wind that is now blowing straight across the pool, and shooting extra line, put in an upstream mend to allow the fly to sink down on the far edge of the current. Even so, I don't think my fly is getting deep enough where it matters. Lower down my fly starts scraping the bottom, and I change it for a lighter one, but I feel dissatisfied with my fishing of the top of the pool. I make a mental note to try it with a heavier line later on, if there is time.

I carry on casting, right down the pool, to cover the top of the Lower Bulwark, which is the only part of it that fishes in this low water, before wading ashore without having had so much as a touch to my fly, or seeing so much as the fin of a salmon. However, while walking up the bank, a small pink fish shows briefly in the fast shallow water between the top of the Middle Bulwark and the bottom of the Upper Bulwark. 'Cheeky so and so!' I think, but cannot hide from myself that I probably fished over the top of it, where with the right approach, I might have had a better result.

I think about trying the medium sinker at the top of the pool; but since the opposition is already fishing the Upper Bulwark (having come down from the Kelpie), by the time I have exchanged the reel loaded with the sink tip for the one with the medium sinker, he will probably be ready to start in the Middle Bulwark, so I decide to head for the Kelpie instead.

I give him a wave in passing, indicating that I have not caught anything, and he returns the gesture, revealing that he too has had no joy. Any audible remarks would have been lost in the rain, which is now coming down harder than ever. I stride up the bank, aware that I am impatient to be fishing the Kelpie, and aware too, that I am actually enjoying the foul weather. Leaving my bag under the stile, I wade out into the river with the full sinker, and 1½in brass tube.

The Kelpie, like so many other pools of this name, is situated at a corner of the river, with the water coming into it down a long slope of shingle. There is deep water around the outside of the bend, and the Kelpie's rock is in the deep water near the top. Even in this low water, there is a strong current right through the pool. The best lie is about thirty yards below the rock, where a fence comes down the bank on the Sluie side. I am fishing from the shingle bottom in the shallow water on the inside of the bend.

I start off at the top of the pool, trying to place my fly precisely, to fish the water around the rock. However, the worsening weather makes accurate casting almost impossible in the strengthening wind, and the rain, too, is coming across the river in sheets, like grey curtains of water. At times the surface of the river is almost completely obscured by the spray bouncing up from the breaking rain drops. Through a gap in the rain, I see the opposition heading back to his hut, unable to take any more punishment. I am enjoying myself. Other than my face and hands, and slight seepage round the cuffs, I am bone dry.

Nothing moves in the water around the rock, and I move down, concentrating hard, and having to use the strength of the powerful rod to force my line and fly out, down and across the stream, straight into the wind. With a little bit of a mend, and the long rod, I can control the speed of the fly nicely as it moves across the slacker water downstream of the rock.

Gradually I move down till my fly is covering the lie opposite the end of the fence. The feeling of keenness and optimism that has been present throughout the afternoon, is still with me. I am therefore not surprised when there is a sudden hard pull on the line, and the reel spins briefly before I can grab it, and raise the rod, to tighten solidly into what feels like a nice fish.

Thump. A pause. And then another thump. And the fish begins to pull the rod tip over. I tighten the drag on the 'System Two 1011' reel I am using by a couple of notches. In the wet they always have to be set tighter than in the dry. The fish moves away from me, and I allow it to peel some line off the reel. It pauses in midstream, and I bend the rod into it, applying side-strain. I move it towards me by about two or three yards. Sure that the hooks are firmly home, I decide to wade a bit closer to the shore into shallower water with less current. The fish suddenly turns and bolts downstream for about thirty yards. As he does so, I move down a few yards and keep the side-strain on him.

I start reeling him back up the pool, into the water opposite me. But he now continues to swim upstream into the fast current, nearly as far up as the rock. I retreat a little closer to the shore, and apply side-strain from my upstream shoulder. After less than a minute of boring against the combined pressure of current and rod, he turns and heads downstream. Reeling in fast, and changing the angle of my rod to throw him off balance again, I bring the fish to a stop opposite me, and on my side of the current. He leans against the rod in a slowly increasing pull, but I don't let him have any line. He stops. I raise the rod and gain a few turns of line. Again he leans against the rod, pulling the tip down, and again I don't let him take any line. He stops. And once more I raise the rod, drawing him towards me, and this time I reel in several yards of line.

He stops, gives a hard pull, and I have to let him go, taking line against the drag of the reel. However, after fifteen or twenty yards he stops, in the middle of the current towards the far side, and again I bend the rod into him, first directly, and then using side-strain by lowering it to my right hand, downstream side, pulling him off balance. He rolls in the water near the surface, although I can barely see the disturbance because of the rain. I reel in fast, drawing him easily towards me. He is obviously starting to tire, although I have only been playing him for perhaps four or five minutes. The pressure from the powerful rod is telling.

I decide that, when the time comes, I will try to land the fish by beaching him. I retreat shorewards, walking him back into shallower water. However, when he is still in a couple of feet of water, he lashes the surface with his body and tail and makes a panic-stricken run for deeper water. This is the first glimpse I have had of him, and he looks a nice fish, 10 or 12 lb, deep and very fresh. I bring him to a stop again, after he has gone about twenty yards, and then start reeling in, steadily drawing him back towards me.

Again, as soon as he is in about two feet of water, although still a good twenty-five yards out from the shore, he panics, and rolls on the surface, lashing the water. I lower the rod towards him, and he heads for deep water, but this time does not go so far, and I bring him to a stop after about a dozen yards. The fish is clearly tiring fast, but is nowhere near being ready for beaching yet. Also he seems very frightened of shallow water, and I decide that, if he panics again while still in a couple of feet of water, I will wade out and use my landing net, rather than risk trying to draw him ashore through more than twenty yards of very shallow water. If he lashes out when in only a few inches of water I risk his catching the nylon leader under a stone, or some other disaster.

Once more I lead the fish inshore, but again he panics and heads out into the river. This time I wade out after him till I am standing in about two and a half feet of water. I now have the fish on a short line, perhaps seven or eight yards of fly line plus about three yards of leader, but it is raining so hard I cannot see him. The fish is diagonally below me, and slowly I lead him upstream, reeling in a bit as I do, until he is level with me, and not much more than about half a dozen yards away.

I pull him round upstream of myself, but he turns, heading down and out into the current. I follow him around with the rod, but he only manages to pull out three or four yards of line before I stop him again. 'Not long now', I think, and unship my net, check the mesh is free, and slide the handle under my right arm. I recover the line, and again steadily lead him round upstream of me, but he stops, and I feel him turn in the water, and then head firmly out into the current opposite me, taking nearly twenty yards of line.

'Oh no! Please!' I find myself saying in desperation through clenched teeth, but he is so tired that he cannot hold his place in the current, and starts to drop downstream. Swiftly I lower the rod to my right, and apply side-strain.

This turns him, and I pull him round, out of the stream and then up towards me. Soon I have reeled in all the line he took, and only the leader and about four feet of fly line are outside my rod tip. He is opposite me, and only about five or six yards out, although I cannot see him yet because of the rain lashing down.

Using my left hand, I move the rod steadily round upstream of me, and grasp the net handle firmly with my right hand in readiness.

The rain is now so torrential that I cannot even see the surface of the river. The spray from the large drops falling so close together is bouncing up about five or six inches above the water surface. Although I can just make out my fly line, I cannot see the leader at all, and I am unable to tell with any certainty which way my line is pointing into the water. I do not know where the fish is, even though he must be within three or four yards of me.

I continue to move the rod round to the left, swinging it inshore. Desperately I peer into the roaring spray, as the rain hammers the surface of the river. There is a jerk from the rod tip, and suddenly I realize that the fish is inshore of me, still totally invisible. Another jerk, and I am aware of the rod tip twisting round. He is downstream of me, pulling steadily. Clumsily, I turn in the river, staggering as I follow him round.

Again I stop him, turn him, and lead him up and gently round inshore. Again, in desperation, I find myself thinking aloud through clenched teeth 'Come on. Where are you?' Suddenly, through the spray, and no more than three or four feet above me, I glimpse the dorsal fin and tail of the fish as he turns suddenly in the surface of the water to head out into the stream again. Swiftly I jerk my net out of the way, lest an outside hook of the treble accidentally foul the mesh as he swims past.

Once more I lead the fish round and inshore, and again I get a brief glimpse, this time of his silver flank sliding by, too late for me to do anything with the net.

The next attempt reveals a brief sight of the back of the fish through the surface spray, again too late for any manoeuvres with the net. However, this time, inshore of me, the fish turns upstream, and I let him go for several yards before bringing him round to lead him back down the stream.

Suddenly, I can see the whole fish, on its side, sliding silver through the spray on the surface towards me, less than six feet away. I slip my net into the river, and all at once, his head, his body, his dorsal fin, have passed over the rim, and he is safely in. 'Got him! At last!'

I pull two or three yards of line off the reel, so that there is no pressure on the tip of the rod, and wade ashore. I carry the fish back up to the stile, and pause for a moment to admire its beauty. Twelve pounds, absolutely fresh, and comparatively short and fat for a Dee salmon; on a day such as this, it is a real prize. Despite the difficulties of getting the fish into the net, playing him only took nine or ten minutes.

I wade in again and cover the remaining twenty yards or so of occasionally productive water below the fence on the Sluie side without any response. Collecting my bag and the other rods from the stile I walk down to the Upper Bulwark. The rain has eased slightly now, and is no longer the torrential downpour of only a few minutes ago. It is still raining very heavily, but fortunately it is now possible to see the surface of the river between the raindrops.

The Upper Bulwark is a fast shallow run, with a number of rocks set in the shingle. It is separated from the Middle Bulwark by about 30 yards of stony rush, and lies hard over on the Sluie side of the river (where I think they may call it the Broken Jetty.) Particularly at the top of the pool, success depends on being able to hold your fly as close to the Sluie bank as possible. For this reason, I prefer fishing it in low water, when the current is less fast, and control of the fly easier. I like to place my fly within a foot of the far bank, and today's strong wind in my face is clearly going to cause me problems.

And so it proves. In the top half of the pool, despite chopping the rod down hard into the wind, and casting as narrow a loop of line as I am able, my fly, leader, and a few yards of the line are often blown back. Only occasionally am I able to achieve my intended presentation. This is to allow my fly to sink as close to the far bank as possible, by putting in a big mend immediately it hits the water, and then letting it drop straight downstream for several yards. Using the long rod for control, the fly can then be swum slowly across the strong current. The further over that I wade, the easier it is to control my fly, as the angle is narrower.

Lower down the pool I have fewer problems, as the main current broadens and moves slightly away from the Sluie bank. This makes accurate placing of the fly much less crucial, and I am happier with the way I am fishing the pool. Three-quarters of the way down, there is a good lie behind one of the midstream rocks, and as my fly passes through this, there is a quick double pull. Grabbing the reel, I raise the rod, and tighten into another fish.

This feels much smaller than the last one, but still manages to pull quite hard, taking out about twenty yards of line, as it heads downstream. I follow, splashing down through the current after it, and narrowly avoid falling headlong into the river when I trip over a rock in the shallow water. Fortunately, rather than carrying on down into the Middle Bulwark, the fish turns at the bottom of the pool, swims upstream again, and is soon opposite me, pulling hard into the current.

I lower the rod to the left, applying side-strain from my upstream shoulder, to pull the fish off balance. I pull his head round, he drops back, and comes in towards me. I reel in fast, but he stops, then shoots upstream and away again. Combined pressure from my rod and the main current quickly prove too much for the fish, so he turns downstream, swimming rapidly, but I pull him off line, and he circles inshore, less than twenty yards below. As I do not want the fish in the rocks and shallow water behind, I lead him round and out into the main current again, getting a good look at him as I do. He is a small fish, probably less than 7 lb, and not particularly fresh.

I reel in, moving the fish upstream with my rod till he is only about ten yards out. Once more he tries to run, but not so strongly this time, and coming to a stop, rolls on the surface twice.

'Won't be long now', I think, reeling in. He circles in down below me, but this time I move back, several yards inshore till I am standing in the eddy behind a large rock. Carefully, I position myself a couple of yards below it, and unship my net, tucking the handle under my arm, and making sure the mesh is untangled. I lead the fish out into the stream, and weakly, he tries to bore away, but without enough strength to take line from the reel. I try to steer him round upstream, but he rolls and splashes on the surface with his tail. I ease the pressure by lowering the rod slightly towards him, and he sinks down into the water before swimming off, diagonally up and out into the stream. However, he only goes a few yards before I have again stopped and turned him inshore, this time several yards above me.

I crouch down in the water, and reel in, drawing the fish head first, directly downstream towards me. With only a few feet of line outside my rod tip, I steer him down, past the rock, and, to his surprise, straight into my waiting net. Playing the fish has taken only three or four minutes.

I raise the rim, with him safely inside, strip some line from the reel, and wade carefully ashore through the rocks and shingle. Everything is much easier when I can actually see the fish I am trying to land. Only 6 lb, and rather pink, I have a strong feeling that he is the small fish that showed in the fast water between the Upper and Middle Bulwarks earlier on.

I fish the remainder of the pool without incident, and then decide to return to the Kelpie. Here despite my best efforts, I have no further offers, and soon it is time to return to the main hut.

Here, outside the door, I notice a bass with a good-sized tail protruding from it. I enter, dripping, to find the rest of the party inside.

'That looks a nice fish', I remark.

'Yes, 14 lb. Bill got him.' This is from John, who gestures at Bill, busy struggling out of his waders.

'Where, and how?' I ask.

'Middle Gannet, on a 3in Waddington. Well, we had tried small flies every way we knew, and nothing showed the slightest interest; then Bill tied this thing on and stripped it in fast across the surface of the water. It was amazing. Fish started jumping all over the place, and he had several rises which missed, before this one took.'

'Now that's what I like to hear. A bit of initiative. Clearly, not everyone's brain cells have been totally softened by the rain!'

John grins, and says, 'Well, appearances can be deceptive.'

Bill, now out of his waders, replies, 'Is that a suggestion that I am not as stupid as I look?'

John, still smiling, answers with an air of injured innocence, 'As if I would imply any such thing. But, of course, now that you mention it, you could always look in a mirror and see for yourself!'

The banter continues while I remove my jacket, scarf, sodden gloves, and waders. There are suggestions that two of the party enjoyed an extended lunch-break in the hut.

'How long were you two down here then? I could smell the cigar smoke up by the road when I came back to the car at three o'clock, and that was with the door of the hut closed!'

'Well, I decided that the only water I wanted down my neck this afternoon had to have plenty of whisky in it!'

'Oh really? It's a long time since I saw any salmon at the bottom of a whisky glass.'

There is a chorus of voices, 'Then don't put so much water in it next time!'

So it continues, and shortly afterward we make our way towards the hotel, for a welcome drink, followed by supper.

Later, when we emerge, it is still raining, but not so hard as it was during the day. The river level has not changed either, still at 1ft 1in. Kitted up once more in waders and waterproofs, I head for the top section of the beat, to fish a pool called the Middle Gannet. This is one of the best low water pools, being deep, fast flowing and rather narrow. However, most of the fish lie on the Kincardine side of the stream, and it fishes well from their bank even in quite high water. There is a line of boulders and rocky outcrops across the river at the head of the pool, separating it from the Top Gannet.

I decide to start with the same 1½in brass tube and full sinking line that I used earlier in the day, and wade out through a few yards of fast shallow water at the top of the pool till I am in position behind a large rock (actually two boulders very close together), shielding me from the force of the stream, at the edge of the main current. In front of me the water deepens very quickly, and I would instantly be swept away if I took an incautious step too far down the slope.

By holding my rod point high, I can just manage to keep my line out of the main current, to hang the fly at the edge of the fast water on the far side. This can be very productive, and at this stance I frequently hook fish with only a yard or two of line out from my rod tip. I lengthen line cautiously, concentrating on covering the deep and slower water on the far side, as thoroughly as I can.

I cast square across the river, immediately putting a big mend into the line, and then keeping my rod pointing up and circling, to maintain a continuously rolling loop of line going upstream, so that my line does not sink down into the fast current. This prevents my fly from being dragged too quickly across the pool, so that it moves through the water at a speed appropriate to its size. When my fly, having fished through the slower water, comes to the edge of the fast stream, I try to hold it dangling there for a few seconds before moving my rod point round, so that my fly first drops slowly back, and then swings rapidly across the current. It is rare for me to hook a salmon on my side of the stream.

There are obviously a few salmon in the pool, because every few minutes there is a splash as one jumps. However, there is no response to my fly from the top of the pool, and it is not till I am standing at least a dozen yards below the rock where I started, that there is a sudden weight on the line, and I am into a fish. I raise the rod, and wind in a few turns of the reel to tighten up.

The fish moves upstream, and I reel in rapidly to stay in touch. It stops opposite me, quite near the far bank, and I bend the rod into it to make sure the hooks are home. With that done, I ease my way back out of the pool until I am standing safely on the shingle. The fish is now on the edge of the main stream, holding steady in the water but giving an occasional jerk on the line. I put more pressure on him, and move a little downstream. This turns his head and draws him into the main rush of the current, where he suddenly dashes upstream, nearly to the top of the pool, and leaps out of the water.

Swiftly I move up the shingle till I am opposite the fish once more, to find that he is very deep in the water, tugging away near the bottom. However, with the powerful rod it is not long before I have him moving again, and a few minutes later I am able to slide him unresisting into my net. A nice fish, 9 lb, and very fresh.

Having carried the fish up to my car, I return to the water to complete the rest of the pool. As I do so I notice one of the Frenchmen, who form our opposition on the Kincardine side this week, walking up the far bank from the New Pool, down below. As he passes he gives me a cheery wave, which I return through the rain, before he starts in at the top of the pool behind me.

As the pool is only a short one it is not long before I have completed it, having paid particular attention to where the water leaves the tail of the pool in two streams, but without further response. As I walk back up to the car, the Frenchman catches a sea trout of about a couple of pounds. I swap my rod with the sinking line for the one with the floating line, and a couple of $^3/_4$in Hairy Mary tubes already attached to the leader, then return to the pool to fish it down behind the Frenchman. Because of the rain and dense cloud cover, it will be dark relatively early this evening, and therefore time to pack up when I have finished the pool.

Starting in the fast water at the top again, I dibble my flies gently over the deep water on the far side of the current. I keep the dropper bouncing and sliding around in the surface layer as attractively as I can, but there is no response, and gradually I lengthen line to cover the pool. As I do so, I notice that the Frenchman is now wading down the far side, as opposed to fishing from the bank, as is normally the case at this height of the water. This is not what I would be doing in his place; the pool is not wide, the fish lie on his side of the current and can easily be covered, with the fly effectively controlled, from the bank. On his side of the river the wading is unpleasant, with deep water, and the bottom composed of large slippery boulders, offering many pitfalls for the unwary.

I have moved about ten yards down from the top of the pool when there is a splash under the far bank. The Frenchman has fallen in! I watch to see what happens, whether I will have to make a dash down the shingle before trying to wade and swim to his rescue, or whether he manages to scramble out unaided. Fortunately, after about ten or fifteen seconds of floundering around, he manages to climb the bank to safety. After removing his waders he empties a large quantity of cold water back into the Dee. Through the gathering gloom, as he ascends the bank towards the road above, I catch the sound of muttering. This I assume to be his Gallic expressions of delight at the invigorating nature of a bath in the clear waters of the Dee. I make a mental note to tell some mutual friends to invite him to join the Aboyne Swimming Club when next they share a drink!

I continue fishing down towards the tail of the pool, but without any further offers. It is now nearly dark, and still raining quite heavily; time to pack up and head for home. I am already planning tactics for tomorrow, if I can get in to fish the pools before the river starts to rise seriously.

This description of my day's fishing illustrates many of the points I have discussed in previous chapters.

I anticipated the worsening weather, dressed accordingly, and apart from my face and hands, stayed warm and dry.

I took three rods with me, one with a floating line, two with different weights of sunk line, all of them sufficiently powerful to cast into the wind, cope with the fish, and long enough to help control my fly.

I noted water height and temperature before setting out, and checked them regularly throughout the day. Knowing the beat intimately, I had already planned the order of fishing the pools. After finishing for the day, I immediately started to plan tactics for the morrow.

The Frenchman waded down a pool where it was not necessary, and fell in. Where needed I concealed myself from fish that might have been lying close to the bank, and waded only where it would improve the presentation of my fly.

Of the four salmon whose capture was mentioned or described, three were caught on the sunk fly, and one on the dragged surface fly. This contrasts sharply with the advice of many authors who believe that the traditional floating line is the only approach needed for low water on the Dee in the middle of May.

I manipulated rod and line to move the various flies at appropriate speeds in different strengths of current and depths of water, rather than adhering rigidly to a single style of presentation.

Staying warm and dry enabled me to carry on with my fishing, and to catch salmon while others sheltered in huts.

Carrying three rods minimised time wasted changing reels and lines; eating my lunch on the bank also boosted my effective fishing time. Throughout the day, I sustained my concentration and motivation, thinking at all times about how my fly was fishing, and how best to exploit the water.

Part 7 — Instinct

Fishing for salmon can be thought of as a way of escaping to more primitive times when man was a hunter in pursuit of his quarry. The most successful hunter is the man who has the greatest understanding of his prey and its habits. This understanding can develop to such a level that it becomes what I call instinct. This is when the hunter suddenly becomes uncannily aware of the location of his quarry, and what it is going to do next, without having any visible or tangible evidence on which to base his knowledge. The phenomenon is not unique to angling, but manifests itself in different ways throughout our daily lives. Generations of modern city living, or the stresses and strains of working life may mask the symptoms, but I think that many people still have this intuitive ability. How often does one hear or read that 'I felt that I was being watched'? If the person being watched did not know of, or hear the watcher, how was the presence felt? The next time that you find someone reading your newspaper over your shoulder on the underground, think about how you knew of their scrutiny.

In other field sports, such as stalking, or walking up grouse and partridges, many people have suddenly found themselves aware of the presence of game before it showed itself. Even in non-field sports as diverse as mountaineering, motor racing and ocean sailing, there have been many accounts of people's feelings of impending triumph or disaster. Anglers are certainly not unique in reporting such instances of prescience. I know that many people would ascribe these accounts to the angler's experience and knowledge, saying that he was subconsciously aware of some subtle shift in river conditions that made it more likely that a salmon would take. Sometimes this is certainly true, but on other occasions I have been unable to find any explanation for that tense nervous feeling that something is going to happen *now,* or that sudden urgency to be fishing in a different pool, or to put down the sunk line and pick up the floating line, or vice versa.

If, on an otherwise fishless day, when I have not seen a sign of a salmon for several hours, or even all day, and I am not approaching any lie of particular note with my fly, and there has been no change in water height, temperature, or colour, nor any alteration in air temperature, wind strength and direction, amount of ambient light, nor any other environmental factor that I could think of, how is it that I am suddenly aware of that 'butterflies in the stomach' feeling, and of concentration at peak level, to be followed a few seconds later by the take of a salmon, the only fish of the day?

Certainly, it is natural for me to become tense with anticipation when my fly begins to cover the waters of a lie that I know to be highly productive, particularly if accompanied by a positive environmental change, such as a period of warm sunshine on an otherwise bitterly cold grey day in March. However, it is not the same feeling as the one that I believe to be purely instinct. Over the years I have grown to trust these peculiar hunches. The more relaxed I am, and the more that I feel 'tuned in' to the river and the salmon, the more likely I am to experience this odd prescience. If I am worried about something unrelated, and not concentrating as hard as I should be on the fishing, then it is less likely to happen.

As I usually fish by myself, it is rare for me to have a witness on the bank to whom I can say 'I think I am going to get a fish in a few seconds time . . . Here he is!' although it has happened. I cannot forget one particular incident when there were witnesses to my extraordinary confidence before the event. It happened on 28 April 1982, and I look back on the incident as being one of the milestones of my salmon-fishing career.

It was a cold, cloudy day with a very strong, chill northerly wind blowing. There was little evidence of fish in the beat, although the river was at quite a nice height of about 1ft 10in. Forcing a line out into or across the wind had been exhausting, and by six o'clock in the evening I was cold, weary, fishless, and dispirited. The rest of the party had fared and felt the same. The wind had been so strong that one unfortunate member had been blown off his feet by a contrary gust while wading down in the Bulwarks. Everyone was so tired from the effort needed to fish in a near gale force wind all day, that we decided not to go out in the evening after supper as usual, but to enjoy a full and leisurely dinner at the hotel instead.

Half-way through the meal, I was suddenly smitten by the thought that I ought to be fishing the Inchbares. Outside the hotel window, conditions had, if anything, deteriorated. The wind was now definitely gale force, with the trees lashing to and fro, and fallen branches being blown along the ground. The urge to go and fish the Inchbares was so strong that I could not resist its compulsion. Pudding was being served when I announced that I had decided to go out again. The rest of the party were more than mildly astonished by my abrupt change of mind. However, enthusiasm and excitement were radiating from me to such an extent that I persuaded two of the others to go out as well. Hurriedly I finished my pudding, declined the previously intended, and seductive temptation of coffee and a leisurely drink after the meal, and left to don waders and coat.

I was standing outside the hotel, doing up my jacket, when Rachel Henley came out. The conviction that I should not only be fishing the Inchbares, but that I would be successful as well, was so powerful that I was already smiling in anticipation. Rachel took one look at this wolfish grin all over my face. 'You're going to get a fish, aren't you?' It was a statement, not a question.

'Yes, I know,' I nodded, still grinning. My friends know that I am never usually rash enough to make such an incautious statement, but this was no ordinary occasion. I knew without doubt that I was going to catch a salmon.

Parking my car, I walked down across the bare field towards the stile. The gale was blasting the fine topsoil from the field in a reddish cloud, but I ignored the grit getting into my eyes and mouth as I hurried down. Normally, after finishing at around 6 p.m., I tie on the flies that I will be using when I start fishing again in the evening after supper. On this occasion, because I had had no intention of going out in the evening, I had not changed them, and I would now have to swap my two half-inch tubes for a couple of three-quarter inch ones. Gripped by urgency and excitement, I opened my fly box a little incautiously, with the result that the wind immediately removed most of the contents. I then had to spend a few minutes furiously scrabbling around in the grass, trying to recover what I could, but at last I was ready to begin.

The wind was howling downstream and a little onshore. I could get my line out across it, but it was a waste of time trying to mend it, or otherwise slow the passage of my fly through the water.

I was no more than a third of the way down the Upper Inchbare when I had my first contact. There was a swift double pull on the line, and the reel sounded briefly. I raised the rod, tightening into the fish. He gave a couple of thumps, and the hook came out. Impatiently I checked my flies. Everything was in order.

I resumed casting, optimism and urgency undiminished. Within a couple of minutes I was into another salmon. This was a nice fish of about 12 lb, but after two or three minutes, the fly again pulled out.

This was disappointing, but I was still gripped with impatience, and the certainty of success. I fished down the pool till I was only twenty yards above the bottom of the Upper Inchbare, and my flies were covering the top of the Lower Inchbare. Behind one of the rocks at the junction of the two pools I hooked another fish. After I had tightened into it, this fish swam straight upstream, right through the pool, till it reached a point level with the groyne at the top. I moved back a few yards inshore till I was standing under the bank. The salmon then turned round, and swam back downstream along the border between the calm water behind the groyne, and the turbulence of the current. As it came towards me I reeled in, and hurriedly unshipped my net. Obligingly the fish continued to swim down the discontinuity between fast and slack water towards me. When it reached a point about four or five yards upstream, I took two quick paces away from the bank, stuck my net out, pulled the rod hard over inshore, and the fish swam straight into the mouth of my waiting net. Only when I lifted it from the water did the fish realise its plight, and how foully I had tricked it. Safe in my net, all its furious lashing was to no avail. It had taken less than two minutes from the time it was hooked till it was in the landing net.

Having resumed fishing, I did not have to wait long, perhaps a quarter of an hour, before I hooked another salmon. However, after four or five minutes' straightforward play, and for no good reason that I could think of at the time, again the hook pulled out.

After rechecking my flies, I carried on, wading down perhaps a rod's length out from the bank, casting into the storm-tossed near darkness. Approaching the bottom, as I made a cast, I had an impression that something did not sound quite as it should, although it was very difficult to tell because of the wind. Suspecting that there might be a slight tangle of flies and leader, foolishly I decided to let it fish round before examining it. A few seconds later, there came a hard pull from midstream, followed, within a fraction of a second by another, and then the reel screamed, rising into a shrieking protest as something big turned, and hurtled down river at high speed.

By the time I covered the three or four yards to the bank, the fish was already about 120 yards below me, and although I flung myself up the steep bank, and out of the river, it had travelled at least 150 yards downstream before I could set off in pursuit.

'Probably foul-hooked', I thought, 'but how could that have happened?' I wondered, as I started to run as fast as I could in chest waders after it. My reel was still shrieking as it emptied at speed, and I was now becoming worried about how little backing I had left, and also about whether the reel would overheat. Fortunately, after I had covered about forty yards down the bank in pursuit, it began to slow, and stopped taking line off the reel. I continued to run after it, reeling in as I went, and brought it to a halt after I had covered perhaps sixty or seventy yards. At this point the fish was a good 250 yards below where it had been hooked. I carried on walking down the bank towards it, reeling in as I went.

After a short time, it turned and started to head back upstream. Gratefully, I made my way back along the bank, continuing to reel in as the fish followed. I had recovered all but about seventy yards of line and backing, and moved about fifty yards upstream from the lowest point I had reached, when the fish leaped, turned, and set off downstream at high speed again. I followed, and managed to bring it to a halt after it had covered about eighty yards.

Reeling in, I closed the distance till the fish was about fifty yards away, out in the middle of the river and downstream. It leaped clear of the water, crashing back in, and then again. It was much too dark now for me to see, but it sounded like a big fish, probably over 20 lb. It moved upstream for about twenty yards, and jumped again with a big splash, clearly audible over the wind. It then headed diagonally upstream away from me, and without warning the fly came out.

I examined my leader. My suspicions were correct on both counts. Over one of the tail fly's treble hook's points was a small white scale, obviously from the belly of the fish. Also, the nylon leader was looped round the back and caught between the shanks of the hooks. It had been pinched so thin that it was remarkable that it did not break during the fight. What seemed to have happened was that due to the wind, or my bad casting, the tail fly and its treble became separated, and the nylon slightly tangled, as I had feared. When the fish took, there were probably several inches, if not a foot, between the tail fly and the entangled treble. With the fly in its mouth as it turned away, the trailing treble was drawn up and hooked it, possibly in the region of the pectoral fins, despite the hook points being at right angles to their normal orientation. No wonder it had bolted downstream so spectacularly.

Resolving that never again would I allow any suspicion of a tangle to pass uninvestigated, I headed back for home. Although I had landed only one fish out of the five hooked, I had enjoyed a most exciting evening filled with drama. However, the dominant thought that recurred frequently during the succeeding weeks and months, was why had I chosen to go out at all, and why had I been so certain of encountering salmon? I could find no logical explanation.

Everyone in the party had made an active and joint decision not to go out, but to enjoy a leisurely dinner together instead. During the meal, conditions outside were even worse than during the day. The others had made no report of large numbers of fresh fish entering the bottom of the beat, or any other encouraging sign. Why then had I been smitten with this urge to fish the Inchbares, but not any of the other pools on the beat? This burning desire, and sudden enthusiasm had been so strong, that not only had I decided to break up the happy party and go out myself, but I had also persuaded others to go out as well. My absolute certainty had been so unmistakable that it had been recognized, and commented on, by others. 'You're going to get a fish', said Rachel Henley. 'Yes, I know', was my reply.

My only explanation for the event remains that of hunting instinct, part of the unseen hand that sometimes guides our footsteps. The more I thought about the incident, the more I realized that there existed intriguing angles to salmon fishing which I had not previously guessed at. This rekindled my enthusiasm for the sport, and my approach to it became far more serious, and thoughtful. In turn, this increased my intellectual satisfaction and enjoyment, because instead of fishing mechanically, I was trying to work out why things happened, what the problems were, and how to solve them.

I have come to trust my hunches, particularly about the method that I should use, or which pool I should fish. Perhaps obeying these hunches boosts my confidence and concentration, and that may help the way I fish my fly. I cannot prove that I would not have been as successful if I had not followed my instincts. However, I have satisfied myself that it is wise to pay attention to my subconscious. Others may pooh-pooh this as all a figment of my imagination, pure coincidence, or a product of my judgement based on the knowledge and experience acquired over many years of salmon fishing. I know what I believe, and that is what is important to me.

Two other examples, the first of instinct telling me 'where', and the second telling me 'how'. Neither occurred in front of witnesses, but both show why I believe so strongly that I am likely to be rewarded if I follow my instinct.

The first took place on 2 May 1984. The river was at 2ft 9in in the morning, falling to 2ft 5in by late afternoon. Apart from a few clouds very early on there was brilliant sunshine all day. I started off in the Slips, and caught first a seven-pounder, and then a beautiful fish of 17 lb. Ordinarily, I would have gone down the pool again, having already caught two salmon, to see if there were any more, but I had a growing impatient urge to be fishing the Flats. I could not ignore it. So I moved down and in the Lower Flat I struck gold, or rather silver. In rapid succession I hooked five fish and landed three, at 14, 9 and 8 lb respectively. The two losses were both avoidable errors. One occurred while I was walking the fish up to the intended landing place, when I put my foot carelessly into a hole in the bank. Trying to maintain my balance, my rod tip had dropped, the fish (in the middle teens) had given a hard pull on a direct line, and the dropper knot gave way. The second had shed the hook while I had been concentrating on freeing my net from its entanglement with an ash branch on the bank, and momentarily allowed the fish a slack line. While all this action was taking place, I had been trying to eat my picnic lunch by snatching a couple of bites from a sandwich and a mouthful of beer, after each fish was landed or lost, and before dashing back into the river for the next. The protracted meal took till mid-afternoon to consume. After the last fish I had a sudden feeling that there were no more in the pool for me, and that I ought to move on down below the bridge, specifically to the Floating Bank. Normally I would go back up to try the Slips again, but instinct had already proved itself to be spectacularly right once that day, so who was I to doubt it? I moved down, changing from an intermediate to a floating line to cope with the slower waters of the Floating Bank. Sure enough, I was rewarded with another fish weighing a bit over 7 lb. After supper, I caught another beauty from the Floating Bank, which took the total for the day to seven fish weighing over 80 lb, an average of $11\frac{1}{2}$ lb per fish. In memory, it remains a day's flyfishing of near perfection. I have never thought that I would have caught so many salmon if I had not trusted my instinct and moved down when I did, and to where it told me to go.

The other incident I have chosen was not so spectacular, and rather more typical of my everyday fishing. It happened on 29th April 1988. After a few bright intervals early on, the day became dark and overcast, with a chilly wind blowing from the north. The water temperature was steady at around 43°F, as was the level at 1ft 9in on the gauge. I started off with the big sunk fly in the Top Gannet, and quickly caught a slightly pink fish of just under 12 lb at the top of the pool. I covered the rest of the pool without further offers, and moved down to fish the Middle Gannet. There was no response, so I returned to the Top Gannet, and fished it down again with the sunk fly. However, while fishing it, I was ill at ease, and conscious that I was doing something not quite right, but I could not identify my fault. A third of the way down the pool, at the corner of the gravel shelf, I hooked a salmon, but I was not surprised when this shed the hooks after two or three minutes play.

Returning to the water with my sunk fly, I was still disturbed by the belief that I was doing something wrong. After a little while my doubts began to resolve themselves, and I became conscious of a growing conviction that I ought to be fishing the floating line. Soon I found myself hurrying to finish the pool, which I did without further incident. I checked the water temperature, which was unchanged at 43°F. It was still heavily overcast, and the north wind was as cold as ever. There was no perceptible change or improvement in conditions. Yet, with my floating line, and two ¹/₂in Hairy Mary tubes I waded in again at the top of the pool, confident that I was doing the right thing. Sure enough, with the fly on the dangle, less than half-way down the pool, I had a firm take. This turned out to be a beautifully fresh sea-liced salmon of just over 10 lb. After landing it, I returned to the river, but my confidence in the floating line began to evaporate as swiftly as it had appeared. By the time I finished the pool, I had become convinced that the floating line would not produce another fish for me that day. In the event I was right, and my only other fish fell to the sunk fly. I cannot prove that the ten-pounder would not have taken the sunk fly, but I do know that I made a change in my tactics in response to my instinct, and I caught the fish.

So, if I have any advice on the subject, it is to have faith in these subconscious judgements or instinct, however you choose to think of them. I do know that the more that I am tuned in to the river, the more likely that I am to be aware of, and to respond positively to these hunches, and that as a result I will fish better, and be more successful. It can mean the difference between catching nothing and catching several fish a day. Confidence can play a big part in making sure that I am more relaxed, and that my subconscious is not clouded by worry or self-doubt.

This communication that seems to pass somehow between fish and angler is, I think, a part of the curious relationship between prey and predator, the hunted and the hunter. It is a paradox that we anglers who enjoy killing salmon, also care more deeply about them than the rest of society. After all, it is the voices of anglers that are the first to be raised in protest at the impact of excessive netting or pollution.

I know that I have a deep emotional involvement with salmon. Having been in the water in a wet suit with them, their effortless, dazzling speed and manoeuvrability is part of the attraction, but I cannot find words to explain it all.

I also know that I do not like to inflict pain or suffering on them without good cause. For this reason, I hate hooking red fish, and if I do hook one, I would much rather it got off than I had to land it, and remove the hook. When I do that, I always worry that I may have injured the fish, and that it will not recover to spawn. Because of this, if 'catch and release' with strict bag limits ever becomes established in this country, I will probably give up serious salmon fishing, and my life will be the poorer. For to myself, unless I am going to kill the fish, I cannot justify inflicting pain on them. I would rather not fish at all than inflict pain to no purpose. Similarly, if I thought that the salmon I caught and killed were likely to be a contributory factor in the decline of a river's salmon stocks, then I would again give up fishing rather than contribute to the destruction of something about which I care so deeply. I would prefer them left free and unfished for.

Perhaps part of the attraction of salmon fishing lies in this curious love-hate relationship, that one can love salmon deeply and still enjoy killing them. It may also provide a partial explanation for the phenomenon of the salmon angler's hunting instinct. The most successful anglers may well be those who care most deeply about their salmon, and therefore understand them best, and are most likely to be sensitive to their moods even if they have no conscious realization of this, and so are able to detect this subconscious identification of prey to predator, and make use of it.

Hunting instinct is an important part of, and perhaps a manifestation of the bond that ties the hunter to the hunted. For me it is an indication of the depth of my attachment to the sport, and to my quarry. Salmon fishing provides an escape from the bureaucracy, incompetence, selfishness, dishonesty and unreliability that make much of modern society so tiresome. It provides a rare challenge, both physical and mental, of glorious unpredictability.

If the hunter loves the quarry he pursues, he will not kill in greater numbers than permitted by the natural regeneration of the stock. Nor will he carry on taking fish, regardless of how many are present, if their capture ceases to be a challenge. On several occasions (the first was as long ago as 1970), I have stopped fishing for the day, although at the time I knew I could have carried on catching fish without effort. When salmon fishing ceases to be a challenge, the fun goes out of it. The true sportsman knows this, and also that a deep love and understanding of his quarry is essential to the real enjoyment of his sport.

Conclusion

The successful angler is usually a thoughtful angler, who tries to understand his quarry. He thinks about the movement of his fly relative to the water and to the fish, so that it behaves like a natural organism of its size at that temperature. He thinks about the river from the salmon's point of view to help him locate temporary resting places, long term holding pools, and the routes followed by the fish as they move upstream. He thinks about why he did not catch a salmon in a pool which he knows to have a stock of fish in it. He knows that to find a solution, he must first identify the problem.

The successful angler pays strict attention to detail in everything he does. All items of clothing and fishing tackle are carefully chosen to meet his functional requirements, and checked before use; shoddy or second-rate items have no place in his equipment. He plans in advance to cope with all conditions, how to fish the beat, and how he intends to play any fish that he may hook.

The successful angler works hard at his sport. He organizes himself so that his valuable fishing time is not wasted. His motivation, and his concentration on how his fly is fishing, are sustained throughout the entire day.

The successful angler knows that there will be occasions when he cannot seem to attune himself to the river and to the fish. He knows that there will be times, sometimes lasting weeks or even months, when almost every fish he hooks will be lost in a sequence of disappointment. He also knows that this is only temporary, and that success will return to him in the end. He will analyse his failure, and, in identifying its causes, will add to his future success.

Only the mediocre angler can claim to always fish at his best.

Bibliography

Ashley-Cooper, John, *A Line on Salmon.*

Clarke, Brian and Goddard, John, *The Trout and The Fly A New Approach.*

Falkus, Hugh, *Salmon Fishing A Practical Guide.*

Knowles, Derek, *Salmon on a Dry Fly.*

Sawyer, Frank, *Nymphs and the Trout.*

Index